THE BIG EMPTY

NORMAN MAILER
JOHN BUFFALO

THE BIG EMPTY

Dialogues on Politics,
Sex, God, Boxing,
Morality, Myth, Poker,
and Bad Conscience in America

NATION BOOKS

NEW YORK

THE BIG EMPTY
DIALOGUES ON POLITICS, SEX, GOD, BOXING, MORALITY, MYTH,
POKER, AND BAD CONSCIENCE IN AMERICA

Published by
Nation Books
An imprint of Avalon Publishing Group Inc.
245 West 17th Street 11th Floor
New York, NY 10011

AVALON
publishing group incorporated

First printing February 2006

Library of Congress Cataloging-in-Publication Data is available.

ISBN: 1-56025-824-1
ISBN 13: 978-1-56025-824-7

9 8 7 6 5 4 3 2 1

Book design by Susan Canavan
Printed in the United States of America
Distributed by Publishers Group West

To a lovely lady—
Norris Church Mailer

CONTENTS

Preface   ix

Introduction   xiii

PART ONE

Generations   3

Protesters, Flag-Cons, and The Big Empty   13

The Problem of Leadership   19

Four More Years?   23

On the Loss of Honesty   25

Therapeutic Protest   29

The People's Republic of New York City   35

Iraq, Vietnam, and Politics in a Quagmire   37

The Politics of Tragedy   43

Central Intelligence   49

The Big Empty   53

Myth Versus Hypothesis   61

The Cost of Kerry's Loss   83

What Took Us Into Iraq?   87

Why Don't We Just Get Out of Iraq?   93

Patriotism   97

American Fascism?   99

Terrorism   103

Environment, Profit, and Karma   107

PART TWO

Courage, Morality, and Sexual Pleasure   115

How Rich Do You Need to Be?   153

Political Correctness and Racism   157

Marijuana   163

PART THREE

Mailer vs. Mailer: A Talk About the Sport of Boxing   173

Texas Hold 'Em   195

Existentialism—Does It Have a Future?   203

God, the Devil, and a Third Party   209

Preface

Soon the World War II generation will be gone. With its passing, we will lose our human connection to a time in America that has been informing our present more than we tend to acknowledge. As we barrel into this new century, it is essential that we look to the lessons learned by what has come to be called the *Greatest* Generation. The men and women who lived through the Holocaust, Hiroshima, the creation of Israel, the assassinations of JFK, Martin Luther King, and Bobby Kennedy, Vietnam, the Civil Rights movement, the cold war, Watergate, and the Iran hostage crisis offer us a perspective in depth on our own turbulent times.

The political consciousness of my mother and the parents of my friends began with Vietnam and the sixties. While there is much to be learned from their experiences, I believe it is necessary to look further back in American history if we are to attempt an understanding of our present state. The difference in age between my father and myself spans three generations, my dad being fifty-five years my senior. His political consciousness was born out of the Great Depression and World War II, and so he passed on to me an understanding of what our country was like during the thirties and forties. My own political consciousness has been forged against the backdrop of the technological revolution, 9/11, our invasion of the Middle East, and the ensuing political and social divide that has cut our nation in two.

The parallels between the rise of fascism in Europe and the current "war on terror" were the primary topics I wanted to discuss with my father. They seem to me to be, in many ways, uncomfortably similar, and I was interested in exploring those places where our perspectives converged and where they divided.

Because the younger generations are more attuned to learning from film, television, and the Internet, rather than from history books or the words of our grandparents, our understanding of the past is more easily manipulated by the increasingly sophisticated political and media marketing techniques used by those who hold power today. This is why it is so important that we have these conversations with the older generations, whenever and wherever we can, before it is too late.

When we consider the implications of using nuclear weapons against our current enemies, shouldn't we ask those who lived through the dropping of the A-bomb what it achieved? The tactical objective of ending the war was fulfilled, but at what cost to our collective conscience? My father has debated the use of the atomic bomb both publicly and privately since he served as a soldier in the South Pacific. Today he says it was probably not worth it. But his feelings remain mixed due to his complicated personal experience with the bomb: Toward the very end of the war, his outfit had been slated to land on a Japanese airfield as part of the planned invasion. It had become clear to Truman that the Japanese had no intention of laying down their weapons and were willing to fight to the death with every last man, woman, and child they had before surrendering to the Allies. The choice for Truman: go ahead with an all-out invasion or give our new weapon a live test? Truman unleashed the bomb twice, and the Japanese quickly surrendered. Once they did, my father's outfit still landed, and upon doing so they saw that they would have been left open to the well-concealed machine-gun posts on both sides of the cliffs, which commanded a full view of the airfield. Every man in my father's squadron would most likely have perished had Truman decided not to incinerate Hiroshima and Nagasaki. Nevertheless, he feels that the mental, emotional, and spiritual toll the decision to drop the bomb has taken on us all probably outweighs what it accomplished. Such are the nuances my father has discussed with me over the years, which leave me feeling mixed, and force me to look at as many sides of an issue as I am able before forming a strong conclusion in regard to any difficult question of morality.

My pop and I have a dynamic relationship. Throughout the years it has resulted in laughs, confrontations, illuminations, many late nights, the occasional hangover, and above all, respect. Our conversations have left me with the realization that my generation has only just begun to reckon with the gravity of the times we are inheriting.

My aim with this book is to share some of the insights my father has given me over the years in regard to the dilemmas we face today. It is my hope that others who are so inclined may find this book useful as we all attempt to develop a historical perspective from which to approach the twenty-first century with our sense of conscience intact.

—John Buffalo Mailer

Introduction

To my son John's description of this book as a dialogue taking place between two generations, I would add that it also deals with some questions for which there are no convenient media answers, and this is true regardless of the generation to which you belong.

Of course we are living in a curious intellectual period. Confidence in the authority to deal with large questions has never been more eroded. It is as if all of us are beginning to recognize that the people who run the world are void of real answers. The old notion with which I grew up was that human nature could be seen as progressive in its essence. That happy assumption is now in disrepute. It is as if we are coming to the end of the Enlightenment, for humankind is no longer seen as necessarily capable of creating a world of reason. Rather, we seem to be expanding in two opposed directions at once—as if men and women are growing more sane, more compassionate, more liberated, and more sensitive to moral nuance at the same time that we are becoming more irrational, more hateful, or more confined within an orthodoxy (that is often murderously opposed to a neighboring orthodoxy). We are certainly more inclined to abstract judgment upon the morality of our neighbor. It is, indeed, as if the world is growing better and worse at the same time.

So, it is also a period when firm arguments are without a foothold. So many of our intellectual taproots now end in decay. "The best lack all conviction while the worst are full of a passionate intensity. The center cannot hold."

Yeats wrote those immortal lines almost a century ago, and its echo is loud. Experts on society, on philosophy, history, ethics, and the meaning of art have little to say that can clarify our universe, shiver us to attention, or prepare our minds for a new era. It is as if the hour of the amateurs has arrived.

If I had happened to come upon this book as a work done by two other people, I would have seen it as a most curious presentation. So many of the largest American preoccupations are tackled here in passing. The assumption behind most of the dialogue would seem to insist that this father and son have as much right to rear up as pundits as any of the top media personages. What would bother me most as a reader is that I would also suspect that they have a perfect right to do so. They seem as bright (and ignorant) as searching (and as closed-minded) as any of the other human presences who are telling us how to live.

Yes, where is the good American who does not nod his or her head in blank despair at his or her desire to believe—to really believe—even a little of what they rush to tell us all the time. So wrong as they come in from the Right! So wrong as they come in from the Left! And the Center which Yeats was so certain could not hold is Corporate Capitalism itself. Anyone who reads this book will know what we think about that. In doubt, refer to the title.

—Norman Mailer

P.S. Because this book has been put together from separate articles and interviews, some of our concepts are emphasized more than once.

Repetitions will certainly occur. I must confess however, that I would like to think that many of these ideas are worth repeating.

PART ONE

Generations

JBM: Although most call my generation GenY, I believe a better label might be the Bridge Generation. I think of us, the ones who graduated from high school in the midnineties, as the last generation to begin discovering what the world was all about before we got hit by the technological revolution and the age of terror. In 1996, the year I graduated from high school, our library had three computers with access to the Internet. There was this tool called the Internet, which could be helpful for research if you wanted to use it, but you certainly didn't have to. In fact, it was recommended that we use the library stacks instead. Four years later, when I graduated from college, you had to register for your classes online. There was no alternative. Get online or get no classes. Everyone had e-mail and a cell phone. The world was suddenly faster and smaller and filled with near-infinite possibilities. It was also a great deal more confusing.

After my generation is gone, no one will remember what the world was like before the technological revolution. No one will have a clear sense of what we've gained and lost because of it. That scares me. But it also makes me feel the responsibility to preserve what I can of the old world, and pass that on to the generation beginning to come up now.

As we continue to move from a tangible to a digital record of history, as more and more magazines and newspapers stop printing and go completely to the Web, the chance of history being rewritten to serve the powers that be increases exponentially. What advice would you give us in trying to hold on to the positive elements of the twentieth century?

NM: As you spoke, I was thinking of the vast gap between your generation and mine. I am your father, but I am also more than fifty years older than you. You're right. That does make me ancient enough to be your grandfather. So, it isn't as if there are two generations between us—rather, it feels like four or five. Not because we're far apart personally, but when we try to address certain questions, our conversation takes turns I don't comprehend routinely. As you know, I can't even turn on a PC. Indeed, as a good Luddite, I make it a point of honor not to use one. At the same time, I have all the advantages of computers because I have an excellent assistant, Judith McNally, and she's been working with me for many years and she loves them. So I receive the agreeable aspects without having to dive into the moil. To me, there is a kind of neurasthenia built into working with the computer. To look at a screen all day is to take one down below the spiritual punishment of those who had to bang away at typewriters all their lives. It's hard to explain how agreeable it is to do one's writing in longhand. You feel that all of your body and some of your spirit has come down to your fingertips. Even if you have bad handwriting, as I do, there's something perversely elegant about it. Then, after you've written in longhand, to see it typed up by someone else (if you are fortunate enough to afford that sort of work) means that you are able to read your stuff as if someone else wrote it. I can move forward as the originator of the text, yet now I am also its editor. I can employ, thereby, both sides of my working self. Whereas when authors work directly off the computer, they are typing and editing as they go, conflating two essentially opposed processes that call upon different skills. That, to me, is one small part of the psychic toll visited on your generation.

JBM: I agree. Personally, I write longhand first. Most of the time, I don't have the luxury of someone to type it up for me. But that does give me a unique edit, which you lose when you don't type it up yourself. I become not only the originator and the editor but the craftsman who turns the idea into tangible reality. There's something gained in that. However, when I do my initial writing on the computer, something is lost. It's too sterile. These are some of the differences I'm referring to. For example, when I speak to younger generations, they don't understand the pleasure of holding a newspaper in your hands in the morning as opposed to getting your information online.

NM: Let me ratchet this up several notches. To answer your question in any real way—to give advice to your generation, my God—I would have to explain that I am now in a deeper state of intellectual pessimism than I have ever been. Mind you, this is not clinical depression. The irony is that I'm probably happier personally, and more composed than ever before. But that's because I've laid certain things to rest. And I still want to keep on working. That's so important when you are my age. Once, at Actors' Studio, Elia Kazan said, "Work is a blessing." I could put that remark up, typed in big letters, over my desk because if all else fails, the work is there, the inner sense of purpose. But that's also beside the point. My larger perspective contains a fear that we may not reach the end of this century. We've advanced enormously. By the measure of previous history, it's as if during my life span, we've progressed not through four generations, but eight, even ten, as if we've squeezed two to three centuries into the last fifty years. As a result, the world is vastly more powerful and yet more sensually deprived. More noise, more din, more interruption in the world. I feel as if we're losing the ability to concentrate. Everyone seems to suffer from a sense that they are getting dim in their memories. Yet, more and more, we in the West are engaged in a race to conquer nature on our terms. That is undeniably a large and general remark, but it's as if back of everything, a great war is going on here, larger even than we realize, between the liberals and the conservatives. The conservatives are saying, in effect, "You guys are trying to wreck existence by becoming too vain, too Godless." And liberals are replying, "Your obsession that God is judgmental looks to force all of humanity into rigid patterns that won't work any longer." The worst of it is that they are both right. It's a war between extremes, and they are both right. Not in relation to their own beliefs and suppositions, but they are right in their criticism of each other. This serves to augment my gloominess. At its worst, I have to tell you, my feeling is that we will be lucky to get to the year 2100. Over the last century, living with our fear of nuclear war, that became a prime worry. Would we even reach the next century? Well, we did. The cold war ended in a most astonishing fashion. After all, given the paranoia that existed on both sides, it was remarkable how peacefully it ended. That could happen again. Life may well go on. But we are in greater danger than we ever were before because we have more power, and we just don't begin to know how to deal with it. The war in Iraq, parenthetically, is a perfect example. When it comes to looking to build societies, we Americans are all thumbs. The more powerful we become, the more ignorance we reveal of the nature of other cultures. I look upon the speed of technology, the speed of communication, and the speed of the Internet as being the most dire factors in this. Because knowledge is now too easy to acquire. In my ancient time (my boyhood), if you wanted to learn something, you had to get up on a Saturday morning, go to the library, pass through a kindly or cruel librarian—especially if you were a kid—and end up having to know how to search for the information you wanted. And in the course of it, you came into contact with books which had their own redolence. You were living in a cultural medium that was resonant. Now, it's electronic.

JBM: Absolutely. When you go to the library, you have a tangible sense of what you're researching. It's all there in your hands. But when information comes too easily through the Internet, it's hard to keep it all straight. There may be endless amounts of text too copious to process, and as a result, we don't know when we've come to a reasonable conclusion.

NM: I would say the Internet gives a false sense of how much knowledge we need and how much we can do without. Because it comes too easily.

JBM: You have a great line about technology: "More power, less pleasure."

NM: Take out "great line." From now on, no compliments. You are my son. You can't go around giving me compliments.

JBM: (*Laughs*) All right, I'll never compliment you again.

NM: Not never again. Just for the purposes of this book.

JBM: When I talk to most of the people I know, they do feel that our technology equals more power, less pleasure. The promise of technology was that we could do things five times as fast, so we would have more time to play with our children and enjoy life. Instead, we do five times more than we used to. There seems to be this anxiety that unless you have your BlackBerry and cell phone on you at all times—essentially a mobile office that follows you anywhere—you will fall behind. How do we overcome this?

NM: Well, I'm out of answers. The strength of capitalism does have its weakness embedded within it. For capitalism is greed. What makes it strong is that there is creativity mixed in with the greed. No question about that. It seems to be demonstrated that capitalism achieves more creativity than socialism. However, it does it at a foreseeable price, which is that greed becomes paramount. Greed becomes respected, and that is the commencement of many new corruptions and horrors. I don't know how you fight it. Because I've seen America dumbed down by capitalism. I've seen our country become more and more powerful economically over these last thirty or forty years, but I've also seen it become less cultivated. Less civilized. And ours is presumably the greatest of all the experiments in democracy. For democracy is always an experiment. But instead of improving, we're getting worse. You could point to our president. Compare him to Roosevelt, Eisenhower, Kennedy, even Johnson. What a fall in stature, in capability, in mental grace. The same is true of the way we speak these days. I have made the remark before, but I believe that one of the treasures to keep England together was Shakespeare. Through all the ups and downs of their history, the English kept a great pride in their language. We don't. We are violating our language. Part of it is hard sell, and our endless advertising. Part of the dumbing down comes from the constant interruptions of our attention on television. Part of the dumbing down is our excessive show of patriotism.

JBM: We do take great pride in our flag.

NM: Fascist countries always exhibit great pride in their flag. Flags make me uneasy.

Protesters, Flag-Cons, and The Big Empty*

JBM: Let's start with *Fahrenheit 9/11.* I've seen it three times and with each viewing, I became more aware of Michael Moore's tricks. I would say about 50 percent of the film is indisputable, particularly the portion on Iraq, but in the first half he uses too many needless devices.

NM: I don't disagree. I saw it for the first time last night, and was upset through the first half. You don't make your case by

---

* The following interview first appeared in *New York* Magazine on August 9, 2004, twenty-one days before the Republican National Convention in New York.

showing George H. W. Bush and a Saudi sheik shaking hands. On a photo op, important politicians will shake hands with the devil. Moore seems to think that if you get people laughing at the right wing, you will win through ridicule. He's wrong. That's when we lose. Back with the Progressive Party in 1948, we used to laugh and laugh at how dumb the other side was. We're still laughing, and we're further behind now.

On the other hand, the stuff on Iraq was powerful. There, he didn't need cheap shots. The real story was in the faces. All those faces on the Bush team. What you saw was the spiritual emptiness of those people. Bush has one of the emptiest faces in America. He looks to have no more depth than spit on a rock. It could be that the most incisive personal crime committed by George Bush is that he probably never said to himself, "I don't deserve to be president." You just can't trust a man who's never been embarrassed by himself. The vanity of George W. stands out with every smirk. He literally cannot control that vanity. It seeps out with every movement of his lips, every tight-lipped grimace. Every grin is a study in smugsmanship.

JBM: His face does bring out the rage of the left. Never before have I seen so many people's blood boil at the sight of an American president. Especially in New York. Of all the cities out there, why would the Republicans pick New York to hold their convention?

NM: I would say they are hoping for ugly attacks. If I were a voice in top Republican circles, I might be offering this advice: "What we need for New York is a large-scale riot. Some of those activist kids will be crazy enough to do a lot on their own, but we can do better with a few of our guys, well-placed, ready to urinate on the good American flag. Let us recognize that if we lose, all we've been doing since 2000 is bound to come out. Back a couple of years ago, Karl Rove was saying that we could gain a twenty-year hegemony by winning the next election. He hasn't said it lately, not since the worst of Iraq came through. Because now, Rove may be saying to himself: We could be out of power for those same twenty years. So I recommend that we put as many of our people into the protest movement in New York as we can find." Or so, at least, speaks the cool Republican planner I envisage in my mind.

JBM: There could be such people out there. But the Republicans may not even need them. There are thousands of fifteen-, sixteen-, seventeen-year-old anarchists, who are truly angry. These kids don't really know what anarchy is all about, but they do know that when they throw a brick through a window, it makes them feel good and there's a chance they will end up on television. This feeds into the celebrity craze that America is under right now of "Get on TV, man!" That's when you're really important. This may be the first protest where there will be as many cameras as protesters.

NM: Some of them will have footage to sell afterward. The networks and cable companies will be looking for clips.

JBM: Right, but it's also for the demonstrators' own protection. A cop is much less likely to bash a protester in the head if he's holding a video camera.

NM: I must say, I hadn't thought of that.

JBM: I feel we've entered a realm where the question is, Whose propaganda is better? The left is beginning to figure out that they can't beat the right with intelligent argument. They need punch phrases that get to the heart of the average American. If that's the case, what is the future for our country?

NM: That's not my first worry right now. Do the activists really know what they're going into? That's my concern. Or do they assume that expressing their rage is equal to getting Kerry elected? It could have exactly the opposite effect. The better mode may be to frustrate the Republicans by coming up with orderly demonstrations. Now, when I was young, the suggestion to be moderate was like a stink bomb to me. An orderly demonstration? What were we, cattle? You have to speak out with your rage. Well, I'm trying to say, we would do well to realize that on this occasion, there are more important things than a good outburst. I wish we could remind everybody who goes out to march of the old Italian saying: "Revenge is a dish that people of taste eat cold." Instead of expressing yourself at the end of August, think of how nicely you will be able to keep expressing yourself over the four years to come if we win. Just keep thinking how much the Republicans want anarchy on the street. I say, Don't march right into their trap.

JBM: What can activists do to avoid that?

NM: Well, the trouble with being in a cautionary position is that you're limited. You're trying to slow down a wave. Everyone expects excesses—it's a question of how many there will be. Most of the leaders of most of the activist organizations are responsible—most of them, certainly. And I think some of them see the peril. They will do well to look at their own ranks, and see if they've got some peculiarly rotten apples in the barrel.

The Problem of Leadership

JBM: One of the problems with this movement is that there's no leader, per se. There are spokespeople for each group. But this is a movement that has grown organically and has relied on the goodness of human nature almost to a fault. And I believe it's coming to a head where, without somebody directing the huge crowd that's going to be there, without saying, "This is what the movement believes in," Middle America will see nothing but anarchy.

NM: You make me think of the march on the Pentagon in 1967. There was a marvelous guy named David Dellinger, now dead, who led it, and a man named A. J. Muste, an old anarchist, also gone, a fine old anarchist. They got together and realized they had to find some kind of umbrella organization that could have input to all the activist groups. And they succeeded. They had a series of discussions with the various elements. And there was virtually no disarray to speak of, compared to what it could have been. The march on the Pentagon even ended up having a final effect that was impressive. I think it was the beginning of the end of the war in Vietnam, and for a very simple reason: Lyndon Johnson saw 50,000 mostly middle-class people come to Washington to stage a set of demonstrations that were going to be opposed by troops and police. LBJ knew people well. From his point of view, most middle-class people were hardly full of physical bravery. If they were going to pay their own money and come by car or bus or train to march into the possibility of being hit over the head with a cop's club, then there had to be millions of people behind them.

JBM: I don't know that there's time to change the mood before the Republican National Convention begins.

NM: I don't think there is, but my hope is there are also going to be enough people whose most powerful passion will not be to get on TV, but to defeat Bush. And you know when a crowd is unruly, simple things can calm them, too.

JBM: Such as?

NM: Such as one guy who has enough authority and charisma to say, "Fellows, let's not blow it . . ."

JBM: There are techniques to stop an all-out brawl that I've seen in action, which have worked. When a cop hits a little hippie in the head, instead of charging, if everybody sits down and the cameras are rolling, whoever is in charge of the police at that given time knows, this is going to look horrible; this is going to make news. But, as you say, you need someone to stand up there and calm the crowd.

NM: It's far more powerful than a good drug; it's extraordinary. It's hard to tone down. This is why I feel dread about what's coming up. I think with all the cautionary words in the world, things are likely to bust loose. If I were a powerful Democrat, I would already be discounting the losses, thinking of how do we recoup. Those losses could be widespread.

Four More Years?

JBM: I don't know that we can make it through another four years of Bush.

NM: Oh, we'll make it through, although I'm not saying what we'll be like at the end. By then, Karl Rove may have his twenty years. Just think of the kind of brainwashing we've had for the last four. On TV, Bush rinses hundreds of thousands of American brains with every sentence. He speaks only in clichés. You know, I happened to run into Ralph Nader recently in Chicago and I, like a great many others, was looking to dissuade him from his present course. He's a very nice man, maybe the nicest man I've met in politics—there's something very decent about Nader, truly convincing in terms of his own probity. So I didn't feel, "Oh, he's doing it for ugly motives." Didn't have that feeling at all in the course of our conversation. Still, I was trying, as I say, to dissuade him, while recognizing that the odds were poor I'd be successful. At one point, he said, "You know, they're both for the corporation, Kerry and Bush." And it's true; both candidates are for the corporation, and I do agree with Nader that ultimately the corporation is the major evil. But in my mind, Bush is the immediate obstacle. He is a collection of disasters for America. What he does to the English language is a species of catastrophe all by itself. Bush learned a long time ago that certain key words—"evil," "patriotism," "stand firm," "flag," "our fight against terrorism"—will get half the people in America stirred up. That's all he works with. Kerry will be better in many ways, no question. All the same, he will go along too much with the corporations who, in my not-always-modest opinion, are running America. At present, I don't see how any mainstream politician can do otherwise. Finally, they are working against forces greater than themselves.

On the Loss of Honesty

JBM: Can we talk about the moderate Republicans' role in this election? John McCain, for instance. He came out strong for Bush. Why?

NM: McCain, I think, wants to be president. He certainly has every right. All the same, successful politicians have to make hard choices. Very few good people can do it because the hard choices are so often god-awful. In addition, you have to smile standing next to people you despise. Even a relatively honest man has to become pretty phony. If you don't know which way the wind is blowing, you're dead as a politician. You can have the honesty and incorruptibility of Ralph Nader, but, as we see, that does not get you elected. So, even McCain must have said to himself, "I could be president. I could be a much better president than George Bush ever dreamed of being. Whereas, if I go with Kerry, and Kerry loses, I'm doomed—I will be a black sheep to my own party. And if Kerry wins, I'll be a lame duck vice president all the way. On the other hand, if I go with Bush and he wins, in four years I'm the logical choice to be the Republican candidate. Indeed, win or lose for Bush, I'm the front-runner Republican candidate for 2008."

JBM: However, if McCain comes out strong for Bush—say, he were even to run as his vice president, and Bush wins, I can't imagine McCain would be able in all good conscience to put up with what Bush would do with another four years. How is he in a strong position to run for president if he kowtows to Bush?

NM: Politicians do have their vanity. McCain might think, "George is an empty vessel. If I were vice president, I could influence him. He might become a better chief executive if I were vice president." That could be the barb on the harpoon that hooks McCain. "I owe it to the country to make George W. Bush a better president." Yes, McCain could decide, "I have to bite the bullet and work for a man I truly despise. But it's necessary. America needs it." The moment a politician says to himself, "America needs it," he can shift the direction of the wind within the halls of his own brain.

Therapeutic Protest

JBM: Let's talk about protest as an end in and of itself. Are there benefits other than the political?

NM: Yes. I think so. People who run protests have a chance to exercise power where they couldn't otherwise, since generally they are against the system in one large way or another. Yet, some of them have serious talents for organizing, directing, and leading. And people who join very often get a good bit of therapy. Literally. They are not only able to vent real rage, but can test their courage.

JBM: Well, they are also doing something about the way they feel politically.

NM: That's the third benefit—a dubious one. You can feel, yes, you're working to change the system, but are you changing it, or confirming it? Never assume that a protest is going to accomplish what you want it to. The middle-of-the-road media interpretations dull the effect, warp it, or even choke it off. If you could talk to the people you really want to reach out there, people far from New York, talk to them face to face, eye to eye, they might listen, because you do have things to say. Of course, you have to stay cool. Americans get nervous when listening to anyone who's keyed up. Major politicians are always cool. The one moment, for example, when Howard Dean went over the top, remember? The media never forgave him. And the mass of TV viewers followed like sheep. Dean had committed a no-no—he had expressed some pain and anger loudly. The media destroyed his campaign on the spin. The problem with protests is that you have to pass through that immense filter of the news media. So you do get on TV for your fifteen seconds of Warholian fame. All your friends say, "Hey, man, you were on" as if you've accomplished something. You might have been screaming. You might have had your face painted with ketchup to look like blood. Even if you manage to be semireasonable on the air, the odds are against speaking incisively and calmly. Because, you've just got the one moment. So, all too often, protests accomplish the opposite of what they desire. Over the long term, protests can do a lot, but not at once. For example, when we had the march on the Pentagon in the fall of 1967, the immediate reaction was bad. The media trashed us. But we did have a positive effect over a period of time. In contrast, the demonstrations in Chicago in the summer of '68 probably lost Humphrey the election.

JBM: Why?

NM: Well, liberals did react against the open, ugly and unforgettable spectacle of the police smashing into the front ranks of the marchers, but even more voters felt that anarchy was loose in the street, so they blamed the marchers for aggravating the cops. A great majority of Americans are very much keyed to public order. We're a country where everyone who came here tore up old roots by leaving their home country. That creates a long-term anxiety. So, in America, the reluctance to cause disturbance is always sitting there in opposition to the other big American desire—which is to express oneself, to be free and free-spoken. I can speak from my own experiences as a candidate for mayor in the New York primaries of 1969. I thought people would want what I offered. But I was opting for too much change. In politics, people want continuance. Americans don't want their lives disturbed. That's the basic problem with protest. It's good for the protesters, but not always so good for the candidate you want to get in.

JBM: Let's go back to the '68 protest. What were its successes?

NM: I think it was not too bad for a lot of people who were in it, individual kids who discovered that they did have the balls to protest. Because when you do, you have to pass through your fear. After all, you can get beaten up. Not everyone can face that possibility. So it could have been good for some of those who forced themselves into the protest, good for their self-respect down the road.

JBM: Don't you think that, in large part, due to the protests, the Vietnam War ended?

NM: That was one large reason. But I've always felt that what made the suits who run so much of America truly nervous, was the notion that they could no longer trust the kids who came to work for them from the best universities. In that sense, protests against the war were serious, were effective. But that's not the situation today.

The People's Republic of New York City

JBM: Would you say New York is part of America, or is it its own entity?

NM: You want to talk about great American cities, speak of Boston, Chicago, New Orleans, San Francisco. Put up your own favorites, if you have any. Los Angeles, if you must. But New York is our only world-city. It does not have a hell of a lot in common with the rest of America, it doesn't even have much to do with upper New York State. Which is why all those years ago I said, Let's separate. I saw New York as eventually becoming comparable to Hong Kong, a semi-independent city-state. For better or worse, it may yet happen.

Iraq, Vietnam, and Politics in a Quagmire

JBM: Doesn't Iraq relate to Vietnam? Aren't we in the same kind of quagmire?

NM: Bad as Iraq has been up to now, Vietnam was worse. We were there in force for ten years. Nearly sixty thousand of our soldiers were killed and two million Asians. What is immediately comparable to Iraq is that the logic for being in Vietnam proved false. The domino theory did not play out. Southeast Asia may have been a mess afterward, but only Vietnam turned communist, and it was well on the way before we came in. The major difference is that in Iraq we have exacerbated the two major branches of a religion that has had power over its followers for more than thirteen centuries. Communism had only been in existence since 1917—fifty years, therefore, by 1967. Its historic roots were not nearly so profound. It is not the size of the casualties in Iraq so far that weighs on us so much as the prospect of a century of unending terrorist acts, which we can agitate but do not know how to terminate by military force. Whether this fear will work to Kerry's benefit, I can't say. The question is, How clear will it be in the awareness of Middle America that Kerry was a combat hero and Bush was a National Guard flight suit? It will be interesting to see how the Republicans will look to tarnish Kerry's war record. Not all Republicans, however. I think a minority of conservatives are ready to go for Kerry.

JBM: You really do?

NM: I've been saying for a couple of years that Bush is not a conservative. He's what I call a flag conservative, a Flag-Con. He's not as interested in conservative values as in empire-building. The classic conservative, someone like Pat Buchanan or, to a more complicated degree, Bill Buckley, does believe that certain values in society must be maintained. The classic conservative believes in stability. You make changes grudgingly and with a great deal of prudence. Don't move too quickly is the rule of thumb, because society, as they see it, is essentially a set of compromises and imbalances that can be kept going only by wisdom and, to use the word again, prudence. So you don't go off in wild, brand-new directions. None of this characterizes Bush. As a Flag-Con, he is surrounded by the tycoons of the oil industry, plus neoconservatives, plus gung-ho militarists who believe that since we've created the greatest fighting machine in the history of the world, it's a real shame not to use it. These three different groups came together on a notion that I would call "exceptionalism." The more ideological among them believe that when the cold war ended, it was America's duty to take over the world. They believe God wanted America to run the world. All too many Americans do believe that. Just look at the patriotic fever every time there's an occasion for people to show their flags. Very few fascist nations ever failed to put a huge emphasis on getting people to wave flags. This is not the same as calling America fascistic—we are not next door to fascism yet—but even as certain people fall into a precancerous condition, I would say America could be approaching a pre-fascistic condition. And the basic notion behind such an impetus, what the Flag-Cons fear, is that America is going to lose its preeminence in the world unless drastic steps are initiated. As, for example, taking over the oil of the Middle East, as well as enlarging our reputation as a superpower to such a degree that China, Japan, and Europe will not be ready to stand up against us in any important way. These Flag Conservatives would argue, I expect, in their private colloquies, that if they don't embark on such steps, America's control of world economics could be lost forever. There are many indications that the Chinese and the Japanese are much more suited to live in a technological world than we are. Our long prosperity has one irony built into it. We have become a pleasure-loving nation. Fifty years ago, Americans were more hard-working. They still believed it was good in and of itself to work for most of your life. That's no longer so true. In science, our college youth are weak when it comes to studying the so-called STEM subjects— science, technology, engineering, and mathematics. Living with technology is, after all, not always so agreeable. And Americans are pleasure-loving. The majority of the Chinese have not had that opportunity. Perhaps they can put up with monotony, boredom, and cruel repetitive working environments far better than we can. No one's ever been able to convince me that sitting in front of a computer all day is a good way to live, especially if you're not using the computer cre-atively to search for new information you really want, but, on the contrary, are carrying out tasks that you have nothing much to do with, other than serving the business needs of others. The exceptionalists would not phrase it this way, but I think they feel the need for America to become a Roman power in contrast to other nations who will serve as our hard-working Greeks. Let China be our Greeks, and Japan, England, even—while we're about it. After all, the Romans used the intelligence of the Greeks to carry out necessary tasks that Romans no longer had the desire to fulfill.

JBM: I think it's no longer possible to take over the world with military force.

NM: Can it be that Iraq is telling us as much?

The Politics of Tragedy

JBM: Let's go back to why the Republicans selected New York for the convention. Do you think they still have hopes of cashing in on the memory of 9/11?

NM: A couple of years ago, New York may have seemed like the perfect place to go, the event had been so traumatic. And there is large political profit in offering emotional closure to a national nightmare like the fall of the Twin Towers. 9/11 felled the two most opalescent monoliths of the American economy. It also attacked the implicit assumption that if you worked for the corporation, you were part of a new upper class. To offer an analogy, let us suppose that in the seventeenth century Versailles had been razed and sacked overnight by latter-day Huns. France would have been emotionally gutted. So it was with us. After all, those Twin Towers spoke of America's phallic hegemony in the world even as Versailles declared the divine right of kings. Many an American male felt gelded by the event. Equally, the average American housewife was desolated by the terrifying possibility that one could work for years to build a family and lose it all in an hour. How could the Republicans not choose New York as the place to hold their convention? Given the heroic deaths of the New York firemen and police, the site will also appeal to working-class votes. The Republicans will certainly not fail to make the connection that the protesters are besmirching the memory of 9/11. But a couple of years have gone by, and we've also learned there are a few things wrong about the picture we've had of 9/11. A new set of conspiracy theories is building. There are just too many facts that are not readily explicable. There may well be room after the convention for the protest movement to look into 9/11 with some critical incisiveness. I am no longer a conspiratorialist—I spent too many years wandering around in the byways of the Warren Report. But there are elements here that are not easy to explain. I don't believe for a moment there was direct complicity. In

America, we don't go in as yet for major political coups—there's too much to lose for the powers that be, and we are still a democratic society. You can't pull off a conspiracy of that dimension without having so many people involved that they'll spill stuff all over the place. (You need absolute control of the press before you can pull off a major conspiracy.) But there may have been a sentiment in the administration—let them scream and squeal over this one—that maybe the worst thing in the world might not be that we suffer a disaster. Pearl Harbor, after all, galvanized America. Without Pearl Harbor we might never have been able to go to war in the company of the Russians. Indeed, Roosevelt was accused of knowing about Pearl Harbor in advance and welcoming it. Well, I wouldn't go that far. I don't think the present administration knew that the World Trade Center was going to be attacked. Still, some odd things did happen that day. Immensely odd. There was more than unbelievable inefficiency. I don't know that the 9/11 Commission did all they could with that. They were determined, after all, to bring in a unanimous report. That always means that the radical ends are cut off. It's like playing poker without the aces, kings, and queens, the twos, threes, and the fours.

JBM: What were some of the odd things that happened?

NM: Well, first of all, the flights themselves. Whenever commercial planes go off-course, they receive an alert from their flight-center. If they don't correct their course, fighter planes scramble to meet them. That's standard operating procedure, I believe. It's assumed a hijacking has taken place. That didn't happen with the first plane. It flew from Boston right into the World Trade Center. All right, you could say there's a great tension that builds up in flight controllers. Day after day you're on the alert. But rarely does anything happen. Past a certain point you can get cynical. You know, "Another asshole's wandered off-course." You don't necessarily keep paying the required attention. That is hard to believe in the first place, but what about the second plane that was off-course? Why were there no fighter planes up in the air looking to divert it? The second plane didn't hit the other tower until seventeen minutes later. That is more than difficult to explain. Especially when no one was fired afterward. Then, there are extraordinary questions to ask about the plane that struck the Pentagon, or the one that crashed in Pennsylvania. Some serious suspicions can certainly be aroused. It may yet become an overwhelming national question. Because, after all, who did 9/11 benefit if not everyone who wanted to go to war with Iraq, as well as all the putative empire builders who were ready for an event that could ignite the nation. Now, the great irony of Iraq, the only good that might come out of all that waste, is that it may have deadened these empire-building notions for a good decade or two. Because after conquering a country that offered so little military resistance, the ensuing cost has been prodigious and abysmal. Temporarily, we have said good-bye to the notion that America can run the world through force. My God, we'd need twenty million young men in uniform for a start.

Central Intelligence

JBM: On May 26, 2004, Al Gore called for the resignation of all administration staff under Bush and Cheney who were most responsible for getting us into the war in Iraq. On June 3, 2004, CIA Director George Tenet was the one to retire (along with James Pavitt, deputy director for operations, a few months later). Why Tenet?

NM: The CIA was miserably compromised. Everybody went to great lengths to say that the administration did not lean on the CIA to produce the results they wanted, but I can promise you, the CIA did not ignore what the administration was calling for.

Bush never had to say to Tenet, "You better do it my way," nor did Tenet say to the next person, "My way or the highway." No, it was all covert signals and a paucity of written record all the way down to the poor guy at the bottom who said A is A but now says, "Oh, yessir, A does happen to be Z after all." People in the CIA are often career-motivated. They know the right thing to do for their career. It doesn't always have anything to do with the right stuff so far as intelligence is concerned. And that you learn quickly. The top people in the CIA got there, among other reasons, by knowing what was wanted from the top. Intelligence in itself is ideally an ascetic activity. Like most ascetic endeavors, it can be miserably corrupted. That's true of every intelligence agency in the world. They all end up doing what they feel is needed for their country, for their own career, for their next immediate step. So, the CIA was abominably compromised by the move to go to war against Iraq. Most analysts who had information that Iraq had very little or nothing in the way of WMD soon gave it up. The urge to satisfy the president became so intense that Tenet, who was probably a good director, got carried away. And he said—what was that marvelous remark? He shot both arms into the air to say, "It's a slam dunk." Apparently, he didn't know that the most electrifying slam dunks are done with one arm, not two. I expect

George Bush doesn't know the difference either. However, I won't try to slam-dunk them on this. They were, after all, looking to converse in metaphor. In any event, Tenet had to get out. It would have been intolerable for the administration to face the discord of the oncoming music if he was still standing at Bush's side.

JBM: He said the biggest reason he was retiring was for the well-being of his family.

NM: Samuel Johnson once said, "Patriotism is the last refuge of a scoundrel." I would add that the family is the last refuge of a politician who's retiring in disgrace.

The Big Empty

JBM: Starting with the WTO protest in Seattle back in '99, a culture has formed around the anticorporate, antiglobalization movement. Where do you think it's going? Where should it go?

NM: A good many people of the right, not Flag Conservatives but true conservatives, can feel in accord with men and women on the left concerning one deep feeling. It is that the corporations are stifling our lives. Not only economically, where corporations can claim, arguably, that they bring prosperity (and, frankly, I'm certainly not schooled enough in economics to argue that point pro or con), but I can say the corporation is

bad for us aesthetically speaking, culturally speaking, spiritually speaking. Just contemplate their massive empty architecture, their massive emphasis on TV commercials, which are a
seedbed for interrupted concentration, and their massive com-
placency about their own corporate virtues. They tend to
flatten everything. They are the Big Empty. One of the virtues
of Michael Moore's movie, if I can go back to it for a moment,
is that you could see all the faces of the present administration,
those empty faces, those handmaidens and bodyguards of the
Big Empty. And then Moore contrasted them to all the faces of
American soldiers over there: innocent, strong, idealistic, or
ugly, but real faces, real people. Plus all those suffering Iraqis.
Obviously, people in such torment are always dramatic and eloquent on film. Still, most of those Iraqis had different kinds of
faces. That shade of alienation from natural existence had not
yet gotten into their skin. They might be hard to live with but
they were alive. Whereas the people running this country are
all—with the notable exception of one guy I'll get into in a
moment—kind of awful. They don't look as human as thee
and me. That's a large remark, but I support it. The one exception, oddly enough, and by this I'll probably antagonize a good
many people, is Donald Rumsfeld. Of that whole gang, he's the
only one who seems real to me. In other words, I might not

agree with him on anything, but he does believe in what he says. It isn't as if he searches for the most useful response he can come up with at the moment to wield or save his power. He's interested in his ideas first. The power is subservient to the ideas.

JBM: What makes you say that?

NM: Because he's real. He reacts. He doesn't weigh his words. If something makes him angry, he's angry. If something pleases him, he smiles. If he has doubts about how the situation is going, he expresses those doubts. In that sense, he's the only one of that coven I'd call an honorable man. Let me emphasize: I can disagree totally with people I consider honorable. But never have I seen an administration, which has had, by that measure, so few honorable men.

JBM: Back to Seattle. Where is the protest movement going? Because it is not going to stop after the convention.

NM: It certainly won't. After all, how much can we hope for from this election? If Kerry gets in, he can repair some of the boundless damage Bush wreaked on foreign opinion. But

Kerry will still be essentially procorporation. No major American politician can afford not to be. In fact, if you outlawed the corporations tomorrow, America would have food famines, a frightening loss of jobs, name it. They are installed for decades to come, and we can't look for quick results. The war against the corporation is profound, as it should be. They are deadening human existence. That, I think, is the buried core of the outrage people feel most generally. There is, after all, a profound difference between corporations and capitalism itself, at least so long as capitalism remains small business. The small businessman is always taking his chances. He leads an existential life. He's gambling that his wit, his energy, and his ideas of what will work in the marketplace will be successful. He can be a sonofabitch, but at least he's out there in the middle of life.

JBM: He's creating something as well.

NM: He could be creating something that's awful. But at least he's taking chances. Whereas the corporation is the reverse. The corporation turns capitalism inside out. The majority of CEOs no longer give their first concern to the quality of their product. Since they have the funds to advertise on a large scale, it diminishes their need for a good product. Marketing can take over by way of language and image. Over the years this has produced a general deterioration of the real value of products for the same real money.

JBM: Well, I agree we're fighting a spiritual war against the corporation. And what we're missing right now is the ability to say, "We can provide for you, we can make sure you have jobs, and food." What they're offering is stability. What we're offering is a deeper quality of life.

NM: To win this war will take, at least, fifty years and a profound revolution in America. We'd have to get away from manipulation. What we've got now is a species of economic, political, and spiritual brainwashing, vastly superior to the old Soviets, who were endlessly crude in their attempts. Our governmental and corporate leaders are much more subtle. Remember years ago, when you were around fifteen, you were wearing a shirt that said "Stussy" on it? And I said, "Not only do you spend money to buy the shirt, but you also advertise the company that sold it to you." And you said, "Dad, you just don't get it." All right, you were right, I didn't get it. But now, I notice, you don't wear logos on your shirts.

JBM: I try my best not to. It's hard to find a shirt that doesn't have a logo these days.

NM: There's one more point I'd like to make. I don't sneer at people who enter protest movements. At the least, it can be good or even necessary for their personal development. But I would like these kids to disabuse themselves of the idea that they are going to have some immediate exciting political effect. If they have any, it could be negative. And if Bush wins, we're a most divided nation. Kerry can put it together better than Bush. Bush can't solve any of our problems. He never was able to. That may be the main reason he looked to empire-building. He had nothing to offer but world conquest. So, if he's reelected, what will he do if things remain bad in Iraq? You'll look back on the Patriot Act as being liberal and gentle.

JBM: I will never look back on the Patriot Act as being liberal and gentle. While the protests will not have a direct, political gain—

NM: You agree with me on that?

JBM: Yes, I feel confident in saying that given the parameters of how we will be allowed to protest, I don't see any way it could have a direct, political gain. However, I do feel that when you're out there, and see all the different types of people who have come together—particularly now with the mixture of groups that will be there—you do get a sense that the spiritual revolution may be awakening.

NM: All right, but if we lose the election, it's going to be a very expensive spiritual education. I would be much happier if the protest movements could spread their activities over the next four years, rather than bringing it to focus prematurely. I don't have a great deal of hope that most of the people involved are really thinking of this election so much as expressing the need to vent, to gain some self-therapy, and to express their outrage at what's been done to them, plus their need to gain power in the counterculture. There's all sorts of motives, some noble, some meretricious. But, it's a poor time to exercise our most dramatic democratic privileges. What we do have over all the years to come is the confidence that we breathe a cleaner spiritual air than the greedbags who run our country, and so it is not impossible that over decades to come, much that we believe in will yet come to be. But I do not wish to end on so sweet and positive a note. It is better to remind ourselves that wisdom is ready to reach us from the most unexpected quarters. Here, I quote from a man who arrived at objectivity a little too late in life:

> *Naturally, the common people don't want war, but after all, it is the leaders of a country who determine the policy, and it is always a simple matter to drag people along whether it is a democracy, or a fascist government, or a parliament, or a communist dictatorship. Voice or no voice, the people can always be brought to the bidding of the leaders. This is easy. All you have to do is tell them they are being attacked, and denounce the pacifists for lack of patriotism and exposing the country to danger. It works the same in every country.*

That was Hermann Goering speaking at the Nuremberg trials after World War II. It is one thing to be forewarned. Will we ever be forearmed?

Myth Versus Hypothesis*

Since his reelection, George W. Bush has been more impressive in his personal appearances, more sure of himself, more—it is an unhappy word in this context but obligatory—he seems more authentic, more like a president.

I would warrant that before this last election he has always been the opposite of what he appeared to be, which is to say that he has worked with some skill to pass himself off as a facsimile of macho virtue. That is not unlike a screen star who has been alcoholic but is now, thanks to AA, a dry drunk who is able to

* The following was a speech given to the Neiman Fellows on December 6, 2004, by Norman Mailer.

look tough and ready on the screen. He never wavers when in peril. He is inflexible.

I would assert that inflexibility is not actually at the root of the president's character. Inflexibility serves, instead, to cover any arrant impulses that still smoke within. Of course, to keep all that stuff to oneself is not a happy condition for a commander in chief.

If we contrast George W. to his parents, it is probably fair to say that his father was manly enough to be president but seemed unable to escape his modesty. Indeed, for all one knew, it was genuine. While at Andover, he must have sensed that he was not quite bright enough for the job. Barbara Bush had, doubtless, more than enough character to be First Lady, yet so long as she was obscured by the obliterative shadow cast by Nancy Reagan, she was seen as not elegant enough. In turn, their oldest son, George, in contrast to his father, was neither an athlete nor a fighter pilot. While at Andover he was a cheerleader. That, in itself, might have been enough to drain some good part of his self-respect. It is not easy to be surrounded by football players when you are just as tall and large as most of them, but are not as athletic. The son, out of necessity perhaps, developed his own kind of ego. He turned out to be as vain as sin, and as hollow as unsuccessful sin.

If this sense of Bush's character is well-based, then one must accept the increment of strength that victory offers to such a man. He now feels as entitled to national respect as the dry-drunk screen star after a box-office smash. One can see the magnitude of George W.'s personal happiness now. The smirk is gilt-edged these days.

In contrast, the woe one encounters among Democrats is without parallel. Just as no president, not even Richard Nixon, was so detested, so was the belief implicit, just the week before the election, that no matter how deadlocked the polls, it was inconceivable that Bush could triumph. This conviction was most intense among the young. Now, the prevailing mood among many young Democrats is not unlike the disbelief that attends the sudden death of a mate or a close friend. One keeps expecting the deceased to be sitting at the table again. Or, the doorbell will ring and there he will be. But, no, he is not there. Bush is the victor, not Kerry. It is analogous to the way people who have been kidnapped by the intensity of a dream have to keep reminding themselves on awakening, "I am not in Katmandu. I am in my own bedroom. There will be no deliverance from George W. Bush. I will have to see his face for the next four years."

Of course, if Kerry had won Ohio and so had become

president despite a deficit of several million votes, the situation down the road could have proved disastrous for Democrats. Kerry, given his 50-50 stand on the war, would have had to pay for all of Bush's mistakes in Iraq. He would then have inherited what may yet be Bush's final title: Lord Quagmire.

The truth is that neither candidate proved ready to say why we are really there. Indeed, why? Why, indeed, are we in Iraq? It is likely that a majority of Americans are looking for that answer, no matter whom they voted for.

Undeniably, I am one of them. I have probably spent a fair part of the last two years brooding over this question. Like most large topics which present no quick answers, the question becomes obsessive.

Let me make one more attempt. I would ask, however, that you allow me to do it through the means by which I think. I do not come to my conclusions with the mental skills of a politician, a columnist, a journalist, an academician in foreign relations or political science—no, I brood along as a novelist. We novelists, if we are any good, have our own means.

What may establish some mutuality with this audience, however, is that we do have one firm basis in common. Good novelists and good journalists are engaged, after all, in a parallel search. We are always trying to find a better approach to the established truth. For that truth is usually skewed by the needs of powerful interests.

Journalists engage in this worthy if tricky venture by digging into the hard earth for those slimy creatures we call facts, facts that are rarely clear enough to be classified as false or true.

Novelists work in a different manner. We begin with fictions. That is to say, we make suppositions about the nature of reality. Put another way, we live with hypotheses which, when well-chosen, can enrich our minds and—it is always a hope—some readers' minds as well. Hypotheses are, after all, one of the incisive ways by which we try to estimate what a reality might be. Each new bit of evidence we acquire serves to weaken the hypothesis or, to strengthen it. With a good premise, we may even get closer to reality. A poor one, sooner or later, has to be discarded.

Take the unhappy, but super-excited state that a man or woman can find themselves in when full of jealousy. Their minds are quickened, their senses become more alert. If a wife believes her husband is having an affair, then every time he comes home, she is more aware of his presence than she has been in previous weeks, months, or years. Is he guilty? Is the way in which he folds his napkin a sign of some unease? Is he being too accommodating? Her senses quicken at the possibility that another woman—let us call her Victoria—is the object of his attention. Soon, the wife is all but convinced that he is having an affair with Victoria. Definitely. No question. But then, on a given morning, she discovers that the lady happens to be in China. Worse. Victoria has actually been teaching in Beijing for the last six months. Ergo, the hypothesis has been confuted. If the wife is still convinced that the husband is unfaithful, another woman must be substituted.

The value of a hypothesis is that it can stimulate your mind and heighten your concentration. The danger is that it can distort your brain. Thoughts of revenge are one example. The first question may be: Am I too cowardly to exercise this revenge? One can wear oneself down to the bone with that little suspicion. Or, one's moral sense can be activated. Does one have the right to seek revenge? Hypotheses on love usually prove even more disruptive. The most basic is, of course: Am I really in love? Is this love? How much am I in love? What is love, after all? To a family man, the question can become: How much do I love my children? Am I ready to sacrifice myself for them? Real questions. Questions that have no quick answer. Good hypotheses depend on real questions, which is to say questions that do not always generate happy answers.

Patriotism offers its own set. For some, it is not enough to wave a flag. The people in fascist countries always wave flags. So, some Americans are still ready to ask whether it is false patriotism to support our country under any and all conditions. Others, a majority, no doubt, seem to feel that one's nation demands an unquestioning faith, and so you must always be ready to believe that the people of our nation are superior—by their blood alone—to the people of other nations. In that sense, patriotism is analogous to family snobbery. Indeed, one can ask whether patriotism is the poor man's equivalent of the upper-class sense of inbred superiority.

These questions can provoke us to ask: What is the nature of my country now? Do we have the right to be in Iraq? Why are we there?

Before we look at the familiar answers that have been given to us by the administration, the media, and the opposition, allow me an excursion. What intrigues me most about good hypotheses is that they bear a close relation to good fiction. The serious novel looks for situations and characters who can come alive enough to surprise the writer. If he or she starts with one supposition, the actions of the characters often lead the story some distance away from what was planned. In that sense, hypotheses are not only like fictions but can be compared to news stories—once the situation is presented, subsequent events can act like surprisingly lively characters ready to prove or disprove how one thought the original situation would develop. The value of a good hypothesis, like a good fiction, is that whether it all turns out more or less as expected, or is altogether contrary, the mind of the reader as well as the author is nonetheless enriched.

A good novel, therefore, like a good hypothesis, becomes an attack on the nature of reality. (If attack seems too violent a notion here, think of it as intense inquiry.) But the basic assumption is that reality is ever-changing—the more intense the situation, the more unforeseeable will be the denouement. Reality, by this logic, is not yet classified. The honor, the value of a serious novel rests on the assumption that the explanations our culture has given us on profound matters are not profound. Working on a novel, one feels oneself getting closer to new questions, better ones, questions that are harder to answer. It's as if in writing novels, you don't assume there are absolutes or incontrovertible facts. Nor do you expect to come to a firm or final answer. Rather, the questions are pursued in the hope they will open into richer insights, which in turn will bring forth sharper questions.

Let me then repeat the point. Novelists approach reality, but they do not capture it. No good novel ever arrives at total certainty, not unless you are Charles Dickens and are writing *A Christmas Carol.* Just so, few hypotheses ever reach verification. Not every Victoria teaches in China.

This much laid out, I am almost ready to leave this substantial introduction to what I am yet going to say. Before I do, however, let me present a lagniappe, not necessary for my argument, but there for its flavor. So I would claim that the most interesting bond between hypothesis and serious fiction is that they both have something to say about sex and the social forms it takes. For a long time, I've amused myself with the notion that the poem, the short story, and the novel can be compared to phases of sex. The short poem, certainly, is analogous to a one-night stand. It may come off as brilliant, or it can be a bummer. A love affair of reasonable duration is, all too often, like a short story. What characterizes most short stories is that they look to suggest something forthright by the end. In their crudest form, when young men write their early pieces, the last sentence almost always has its echo of: "He felt old, and sad, and tired." By analogy, it may be fair to say that few affairs come to an end without being characterized—usually uncharitably—by the participants. Marriage, however, like a novel, is closer to a metamorphosis of attitudes. The end of one chapter may leave the husband and wife ready to break up; they cannot bear each other. In the morning, which commences the next chapter, they discover to their mutual surprise that they are back in the sack. Reality varies from chapter to chapter.

I expect I have used this little excursion to suggest that those of us who do not hold fundamental beliefs often approach our sense of reality by way of our working hypotheses, or by our various literary forms. It is certainly true that on the road to Iraq, we were offered more than a few narratives for why we were so obviously hell-bent for war.

In the beginning, some said that George W. Bush was trying to validate his father by occupying Baghdad—others argued that he wished to appear superior to George H. W. Two opposed hypotheses. Each made a neat one-page article for one or another magazine.

Another hypothesis which soon arose was that such a war would be evil. Shed no blood for oil. That became the cry. Quite likely, it was correct in part, at least, but it was as harsh in argument as the prose of any ill-written tract. Others offered a much more virtuous reason: conquering Iraq would democratize the Middle East. Problems between Israel and Palestine could be happily settled. In the event, this proved to be nearer to Grimm's fairy tales than a logical proposition.

In its turn, the administration presented us with weapons of mass destruction. That lived in the American mind like an intelligence thriller. Would we locate those nightmares before they blew us up? It became the largest single argument for going to war. Colin Powell put his political honor on the chopping block for that assertion. He is still holding his head in his hands.

There were other hypotheses—would we or would we not find Osama bin Laden? Which became a short story like "The Tiger and the Lady"—no ending. On the eve of war, there was a blood-cult novel in the night. It was Shock and Awe—had we driven a quick stake through the heart of Saddam Hussein? Good Americans could feel they were on the hunt for Dracula.

Vivid hypotheses. None held up. We did not learn then and we still do not begin to agree why we embarked on this most miserable of wars. Occam's Razor does suggest that the simplest explanation which is ready to answer a variety of separate questions on a puzzling matter has a great likelihood of being the most correct explanation. One answer can emerge then from the good bishop's formula: it is that we marched into a full-sized war because it was the simplest solution the president and his party could find for the immediate impasse in which America found itself. (Besides, a war would authenticate his Florida presidency.) Yes, how much we needed a solution to our developing problems.

The first problem, which could yet become the most worrisome, was that the nation's scientific future, and its technological skills, seemed to be in distress. American students at STEM studies—S-T-E-M: science, technology, engineering, and mathematics—no longer appeared to be equal to those Asian and European students who were also studying advanced courses at our universities. For pleasure-loving American students, STEM subjects may have seemed too difficult, too unattractive. Moreover, the American corporation was now ready to outsource its own future, even eager to do so. Given drastically lower factory wages in Third World countries, there may have appeared no alternative to maintain large profits. All the same, if American factory jobs were now in danger of disappearing, and our skills at technology were suffering in comparison to Europe and to Asia, then relations between American labor and the corporation could go on tilt. That was not the only storm cloud over the land.

Back in 2001, back before 9/11, the divide between pop culture and fundamentalism was gaping. In the view of the religious right, America was becoming heedless, loutish, irreligious, and blatantly immoral. Half of all American marriages were ending in divorce. The Catholic Church was suffering a series of agonizing scandals. The FBI had been profoundly shaken by moles in their woodwork who worked for the Soviets and a Mafia killer on close terms with their own agents on the scene.

Posed with the specter of a superpower, our own superpower, economically and spiritually out of kilter, the best solution seemed to be war. That would offer an avenue for recapturing America—not, mind you, by unifying the country, not at all. By now, that was close to impossible. Given, however, that the country was deeply divided, the need might be to separate it further in such a way that one's own half could become much more powerful. For that, Americans had to be encouraged to live with all the certainties of myth while bypassing the sharp edge of inquiry demanded by hypothesis.

The difference is crucial. A hypothesis opens the mind to thought, to comparison, to doubt, to the elusiveness of truth. If this country was founded in great part on the notion that enough people possessed enough goodwill, and enough desire for growth and discovery to prosper, and this most certainly included spiritual and intellectual discovery, then, or so went the premise, democracy could thrive more than monarchy or theocracy.

Of course, all these political forms depend on their myths. Myths are tonic to a nation's heart. Once abused, however, they are poisonous. For myths are frozen hypotheses. Serious questions are answered by declaration and will not be re-opened. The need is for a morality tale at a child's level. Good will overcome a dark enemy. For the Bush administration, 9/11 came as a deliverance. The new myth even bore some relation to reality. There was no question that Islamic terrorists were opposed to all we stood for, good or bad. They did call us the Great Satan. But even this was not enough. The danger presented by this enemy had to be expanded. Our paranoia had to be intensified. We were encouraged to worry about the security of every shopping mall in America. To oppose the fears we generated in ourselves, we had to call on our most dynamic American myths. We had had, after all, a lifetime of watching action films.

The possibility of weeding terrorists out through interna-tional police action never came into real question. We needed much more than that. War is, obviously, a mightier rallying ground than a series of local police actions. Yet, half of America was opposed to our advance toward war with Iraq. Half of us were asking one way or another: "How much goodness has America brought to the world? How much has it exploited the world?"

The president, however, had his own imperatives. Keep

America fixed on myth. So he went all the way back to Cotton Mather. We must war constantly against the invisible kingdom of Satan. Stand at Armageddon and battle for the land. This was fortified by a belief which many Republicans, some of the most intelligent and some of the most stupid, accepted in full. It was the conviction that America was exceptional, and God had a special interest in America. God wanted us to be a land superior to other nations, a realm to lift His vision into greater glory. So, the myth of the frontier, which demanded a readiness to fight without limit, became part of our exceptionalism. "Do what it takes." No matter how deeply one was embedded in near to inextricable situations, one would complete the job—"Bring 'em on." The myth was crucial to the Bush administration. The last thing it needed was to contend with anything like a real approach to reality.

This attempt to take over the popular American mind has certainly not been unsuccessful, but it does generate a new and major hypothesis which would argue that the people of the U.S. were systematically, even programmatically, deluded from the top down. Karl Rove was there to recognize that there were substantial powers to be obtained by catering to stupid stubborn people, and George W. Bush would be the man to harvest such resources. George W. understood stupid people well. They were not dumb, their minds were not physically crippled in any way. They had chosen to be stupid because that offered its own kind of power. To win a great many small contests of will, they needed only to ignore all evidence. Bright people would break down trying to argue with them. Bush knew how to use this tool. With a determination that only profound contempt for the popular mind can engender, we were sold the notion that this war would be honorable, necessary, self-protective, decent, fruitful for democracy, and dedicated to any and all forms of human goodness. I would suggest that there was close to zero sincerity at the top. The leaders of this country who forced the war through were neither idealistic nor innocent. They had known what they were doing. It was basic. Do what it takes. They had decided that if America was to be able to solve its problems, then the country had to become an empire. For American capitalism to survive, exceptionalism rather than cooperation with other advanced nations had become the necessity. From their point of view, there had been ten lost years of initiatives, ten years in the cold, but America now had an opportunity to cash in again on the great bonanza that had fallen its way in 1991 when the Soviet Union went bankrupt in the arms race. At that point, or so believed the exceptionalists, America could and should have taken over the world and thereby safeguarded our

economic future for decades at least with a century of hegemony to follow. Instead, these exceptionalists had been all but
consumed with frustration over what they saw as the labile pussy-
footing of the Clinton administration. Never have liberals been
detested more. But now, at last, 9/11 had provided an opportunity for America to resolve some problems. Now America
could embark on the great adventure of empire.

These exceptionalists also happened to be hardheaded real-
ists. They were ready to face the fact that most Americans
might not have any real desire for global domination. America
was pleasure-loving, which, for exceptionalist purposes, was
almost as bad as peace-loving. So, the invasion had to be presented with an edifying narrative. That meant the alleged
reason for the war had to live in utter independence of the
facts. The motives offered to the American public need not
have any close connection to likelihoods. Fantasy would serve.
As, for example, bringing democracy to the Middle East. Pro-
tecting ourselves against weapons of mass destruction. These
themes had to be driven home to the public with all the para-
phernalia of facts, supposed confirmative facts. For that, who
but Colin Powell could serve as the clot-buster? So, Powell was
sold a mess of missile tubes by the CIA. Of course, for this to
work, the CIA also had to be compromised.

So we went forward in the belief that Iraq was an immediate threat, and were told that hordes of Iraqis would welcome us with flowers. Indeed, it was our duty as good Americans to bring democracy to a country long dominated by an evil man.

Democracy, however, is not an antibiotic to be injected into a polluted foreign body. It is not a magical serum. Rather, democracy is a grace. In its ideal state, it is noble. In practice, in countries that have lived through decades and centuries of strife and revolution and the slow elaboration of safeguards and traditions, democracy becomes a political condition which can often withstand the corruptions and excessive power-seeking of enough humans to remain viable as a good society.

It is never routine, however, never automatic. Like each human being, democracy is always growing into more or less. Each generation must be alert to the dangers that threaten democracy as directly as each human who wishes to be good must learn how to survive in the labyrinths of envy, greed, and the confusions of moral judgment. Democracy, by the nature of its assumptions, has to grow in moral depth, or commence to deteriorate. So, the constant danger that besets it is the unadmitted downward pull of fascism. In all of us there is not only a love of freedom, but a wretchedness of spirit that can look for its opposite—as identification with the notion of order and control from above.

The real idiocy in assuming that democracy could be brought to Iraq was to assume that its much-divided people had not been paying spiritually for their compromises. The most evil aspect of fascism is that all but a few are obliged to work within that system or else their families and their own prospects suffer directly. So the mass of good people in a fascist state are filled with shame, ugly memories of their own small and occasionally large treacheries, their impotence, and their frustrated hopes of revenge. Willy-nilly, their psyches are an explosive mess. They are decades away from democracy. There is no quick fix. Democracy has to be earned by a nation through its readiness for sacrifice. Ugly lessons in survival breed few democrats.

It is all but impossible to believe that men as hard-nosed, inventive, and transcendentally cynical as Karl Rove or Dick Cheney, to offer the likeliest two candidates at hand, could have believed that quick democracy was going to be feasible for Iraq.

We are back to oil. It is a crude assertion, but I expect Cheney, for one, is in Iraq for just that reason. Without a full wrestler's grip on control of the oil of the Middle East, America's economic problems will continue to expand. That is why we will remain in Iraq for years to come. For nothing will be gained if we depart after the new semioppressive state is cobbled together. Even if we pretend it is a democracy, we will have only a nominal victory. We will have gone back to America with nothing but the problems which led us to Iraq in the first place plus the onus that a couple of hundred billion dollars were spent in the quagmire.

Let me make an attempt to enter Cheney's mind. I think, as he sees it, it will be crucial to hang in at all costs. New sources of income are going to be needed, new trillions, if for nothing else than to pay for the future social programs that will have to take care of the humongously large labor force that will remain endemically jobless because of globalism. That may yet prove to be the final irony of compassionate conservatism. It will expand the role of government even as it searches for empire.

Cheney's looming question will be then how to bring off some sizable capture of Iraq's oil profits. Of course, he is no weak man, he is used to doing what it takes, no matter how it smells, he is full of the hard lessons passed along by the collective wisdom of all those Republican bankers who for the last 125 years have been foreclosing on widows who cannot keep up with the mortgage on the farm. Cheney knows. You cannot stop a man who is never embarrassed by himself—Cheney will be full of bare-faced virtue over why—for the well-being of all—we have to help the Middle East to sell its oil properly. We will deem it appropriate that the Europeans are not to expect a sizable share since, after all, they do not deserve it, not given their corrupt deals with Hussein under so-called UN supervision. Yes, Cheney will know how to sell the package for why we are still in Iraq, and Rove will be on his flank, guiding Bush on how to lay it out for the American people.

It seems to me that if the Democrats are going to be able to work up a new set of attitudes and values for their future candidates, it might not be a bad idea to do a little more creative thinking about the question for which they have had, up to now, naught but puny suggestions—which is, How do you pick up a little of the fundamentalists' vote?

If by 2008, the Democrats hope to come near to a meaningful fraction of such voters, they will have to find candidates and field workers who can spread the word down south—that is, find the equivalent of Democratic missionaries to work on all those good people who may be in awe of Jehovah's wrath, but love Jesus, love Jesus so much more. Worked upon with enough zeal, some of the latter might come to recognize that these much-derided liberals live much more closely than the Republicans in the real spirit of Jesus. Whether they believe every word of Scripture or not, it is still these liberals rather than the Republicans who worry about the fate of the poor, the afflicted, the needy, and the disturbed. These liberals even care about the well-being of criminals in our prisons. They are more ready to save the forests, refresh the air of the cities, and clean up the rivers. It might be agonizing for a good fundamentalist to vote for a candidate who did not read the Scriptures every day, yet some of them might yet be ready to say, "I no longer know where to place my vote. I have joined the ranks of the undecided."

More power to such a man. More power to all who would be ready to live with the indecision implicit in democracy. It is democracy, after all, which first brought the power and virtue of good questions to the attention of the people rather than restricting the matter to the upper classes.

Long may good questions prevail.

The Cost of Kerry's Loss

JBM: In "Myth Versus Hypothesis," you say that if Kerry had been elected, it may have proved disastrous for the Democrats.

NM: Yes.

JBM: Now, eight months after the election, in light of Supreme Court Justices retiring on this president's watch, do you still feel that in the long run it's better for the Democrats that Kerry did not win?

NM: It may be that the price we'll pay with the Supreme Court will prove too large. But my strongest feeling is that if Kerry had won, he would have reaped all the bad cess of the war in Iraq. All the blame. The Republicans would have been claiming, "We had a winning situation until the Democrats came in." The shame, the ignominy, the humiliation of that venture in Iraq would all have been laid on Kerry. Now, at least, Bush is beginning to pay for his sins rather than passing them on to Iron-Jaw John. On the other hand, the Democrats deserved to lose. They offered a dreadful presidential campaign.

JBM: Painful.

NM: Painful, stupid, slack, and soft. They didn't bite the bullet. They didn't come down on that war in Iraq; they went along with it.

JBM: Dean was the only one who attacked the war flat-out, and look what happened to him. Although I found out recently that when Dean gave his famous "howl" and came off as a lunatic, in truth, the audience was screaming at the top of their lungs. Dean was simply trying to yell over them, but the audience was not miked. So over the TV screen, only Dean was heard. I'm wondering, how did his staff fail to warn him that he was on a standard network feed?

NM: Recognize that a candidate's staff is under enormous strain when they're campaigning. There are eighty-five things you have to think about and maybe your brain, which is getting more and more run-down, is still keeping up with seventy-five of the eighty-five details. Lo and behold, disasters occur. You make terrible mistakes. I was an amateur when I ran for mayor but I made a few really large errors, let me tell you. So I felt a certain sympathy for Dean. He'd been under this huge pressure for months and so were his people. Maybe even more so. The exhaustion of a political campaign can be analogous to trench warfare.

What Took Us Into Iraq?

JBM: I know you've answered this in a number of ways, but it just can't be asked enough. Why are we in Iraq? I cannot believe that Bush and Company are a gaggle of fools, not by a long shot. They are the most calculating administration I've encountered in my life.

NM: I like that. The most calculating administration. Yes. Lots of know-how, and no honorable ethic.

JBM: Given their intelligence, how could this administration not have anticipated the long haul of this war? By now, they have changed their reasons for the invasion so many times, Americans are getting hip to the fact that, at the very least, Saddam Hussein posed no significant threat to our national security. This war is developing into an extraordinary political cost for the administration. Why was it worth it to them? It can't just be the oil. Oil prices are up. How does this supposedly Christian administration justify the hordes of innocent people killed—

NM: Come on, man, save time. These administration honchos are very, very intelligent with what they are intelligent at, but they're stupid as sludge where they are stupid. I will say this characterizes almost all political regimes. Take Camelot. As open and bright and quick as the Kennedy administration proved to be, look at how wrong they were on the Bay of Pigs. Why? Because they didn't know a lot about Cuba when they came into office, so they listened to Allen Dulles and the CIA. It was a very painful lesson, but they learned that the CIA wasn't always right.

OK, all I'm getting at is the Bushies in the wake of the 2000 election had a host of problems for which war could be a pro-tem solution. The novelist in me would even warrant that the cynics among the Bush honchos loved the idea of selling America on bringing democracy to Iraq. They may even have known they were not going to succeed on any real level. But they did have great faith in the stupidity of the American people. So, they assumed they could carry it off one way or another. With our mighty military, how could they not find something they could paint as a positive?

JBM: I was twenty-four years old at the time, a writer/actor in LA, and *I* saw what was going to happen if we invaded. How could *they* not have seen it? It's hard for me to believe that they didn't know Iraq would turn into a quagmire.

NM: Listen, these are men who have been successful all their lives. They've gone through many crises. Their feeling is, "Yes, there's going to be trouble. A lot of shit will hit the fan, a good deal is probably going to go wrong. But we will handle it." Not Bush, but Rove, Cheney, Rumsfeld. Take a guy like Cheney. His whole attitude is: "Can do. Will do." I would say their honcho feeling goes like this: "We'll take the sludge that comes our way, but it will be a lot better than chasing bin Laden all over Afghanistan and Pakistan. That won't do it. The Democrats will be too ready to carp about everything that's going wrong in America. So let's shift the war to Iraq. This country is so patriotic. 9/11 brought us back again to operating speed and now we can coast on that patriotism." You have to understand the depth and breadth of the cynical optimism these guys possess. They are able to live with very bad odors, spiritual stinks most of us can't endure. Their strength is in their ability to avoid bad conscience. Immoral is not even a word to apply to these guys. Amoral is no better. They have a God-given or diabolically driven capacity to live with bad conscience. They really don't give a damn. "Hey," goes their credo, "I'm tough. So I can live with this. Others couldn't, but I can take it. I will endure. And even if it don't work, it will work anyway, because we will always be able to find a slew of spokesmen, even intelligent people, who will claim that democracy is beginning to work in Iraq. All those neocons. They keep saying that the Middle East is ready for democracy. Well, I think they are a bunch of Israel-serving, self-serving sons of bitches myself, but if they are right, then we get the oil, and if they're wrong, we'll yet be able to blame them for the consequences." So, yes, John, to speak for myself again, I take them seriously. As they saw it in 2001, the country was in bad shape and they needed a tool big-time to clear it up, especially when they were bound and determined to send all that tax money upstairs to the rich.

JBM: So, instead, they send the poor to die in Iraq.

NM: Don't you think that is one of the themes of history, which repeats itself over and over?

JBM: My question is, Why is that chain never broken?

NM: The reason may be that there are too many strong and skilled people who spend their lives working to keep the chain intact. They labor at it reverently. So they succeed in keeping the majority stupid, even if in a democracy it's just fifty-two percent of the voting populace. They know so well that stupidity is their greatest asset, their political mojo. They work, systematically, to enhance it. They take pride in generating more and more stupidity even as advertising men take pride in selling a piece of crap. After all, anyone can market a Rolls Royce. But try palming off sleaze on a big scale. Hell, yeah! "Bring 'em on."

Why Don't We Just Get Out of Iraq?

JBM: What would happen if we left Iraq tomorrow?

NM: Well, to begin with, you can't. The close argument comes down to how fast could you pull out. Three months? Six months? A year? There is no schedule right now for a pullout because there is nobody in power to make such a choice. There's too striking a possibility that Iraq would break down completely into civil war. You also have the real possibility that Iran would move forces into Iraq to join the Shiites. Syria might help the Sunnis. We might even have to go back again.

And if Iraq divided more or less peacefully into three new countries, you would then have to deal with the hordes of Shiites and Sunnis who have lived in Kurdistan for centuries. But now they may want to get out. Not all, but a good many. You'd certainly have Shiites in exodus from a Sunni area, and Sunnis evacuating Shiite territories. The ethnic unresolvables that ravaged Yugoslavia would be back again doubled.

Now add our own American aversion to looking awful on the world stage. In such circumstances, how could Bush find a new cliché to make his day? We, so great a democracy, have demonstrated already that we have little real comprehension of democracy itself. We don't seem to understand that it has to be built from the ground up, from the inner midnight will of the people who live in that country. No external power can offer you democracy as a gift. If you are not willing to die for your own idea of democracy, then you are not going to have one. But we moved in on Iraqis who were tarnished with the shame of having lived under Saddam Hussein for thirty years. Each of them at their own level, however they saw themselves, had been obliged to make their compromises with the state. Just as you or I would have to do the same if we were living in a totalitarian environment. What may be most awful about totalitarianism is that it sullies everyone who lives under it. So, it doesn't make for nicer people, but for uglier ones. Russia, after the Soviet Union broke down, is one example— corruption and greed came roaring to the fore. You don't just "inject" democracy. You can't. But the administration decided, or pretended to decide, that we could. Now, we are paying the price. We are squatting in the quagmire. No surprise then if we don't know how to keep the splatter off our boots.

Of course, there is also the possibility that pulling out of Iraq would not be a disaster. The void left by our withdrawal might soothe some of the insurgents and could expedite many an Iraqi into feeling a real sense of the need for national unity. There could even be an economic window for growth. More than one European country, at present closed out, might be gung-ho to invest. The Iraqis might resent the profits taken by other countries like France or Germany less than any we could extract. Needless to add, our economic interests would be directly embarrassed. Obviously, to leave now would take moral courage on Bush's part. Which is the first of the many fine virtues he is lacking.

There is one great example of giving up on a bad war. That was the peace General De Gaulle made with Algeria. But it did take a leader of his stature. He had, after all, been the leading proponent of Free France during the German occupation. In contrast, what does Bush represent? An ability to obtain leisurely service in the National Guard and not be called to Vietnam. Now, he tries to personify his idea of a real soldier—ramrod spine. The one thing he can never say is, "I fucked up." That is why we are not going to pull out tomorrow.

Patriotism

JBM: In "Myth Versus Hypothesis," you draw a distinction between two types of patriots: those who are still ready to ask whether it's acceptable to support our country under any and all conditions, and those who feel our nation demands an unquestioning faith. You say the latter are the majority. How much of a majority?

NM: I would guess two-thirds. The fight now in America as I see it—the primal fight, if you will, the one that underlies all the others—is the level of American intelligence. Is it going to improve or deteriorate? A democracy depends upon the intelligence of its people. By that, I don't mean literary intelligence or even verbal intelligence. Rather, it is a readiness to look into the face of difficult questions and not search for quick answers. You can measure real intelligence by that ability to live with a difficult question. And patriotism gobbled up, sentimentalized, and thereby abased is one of the most powerful single forces to proliferate stupidity.

JBM: Do you think the minority patriots, the ones who still hold on to some hope that it's not all lost, are kidding themselves?

NM: I don't know. We're not necessarily headed for disaster, but we may be. I don't know much about the Greeks, but the little I have learned about them in recent years does inspire some respect on this matter. Because they saw life as a dynamic mixture of hope and despair. In other words, you never live without the possibility that disaster may be near. That's part of the human condition. Any attempt to wipe out one's fear of the possibility of disaster is totalitarian, and this is a spectrum that extends all the way from political correctness over to the worst of Hitler.

We are not living with a guarantee of the happy ending. Anyone who purveys such a notion is not working for humanity, but against it. I would go so far as to say that.

American Fascism?

NM: You know, under all of my remarks rest a very unhappy premise. Fascism may be more to the tastes of the ruling powers in America than democracy. That doesn't mean we will become a fascist country tomorrow. There are any number of extensive forces in America that would resist it. On the other hand there are also huge forces in America that are promoting fascism one way or another.

JBM: How similar is America today to Germany in the early thirties before the Nazis took power?

NM: Different. Very different. I sneer at people who say we are now comparable to Germany in the thirties. The difference is immense. Germany was suffering through absolute demoralization. The profound insult of the Versailles Treaty hung over them. Both sides had been equally guilty in starting that war, but they were made the sole criminals. They saw that as an outrage. The reparations they had to pay were extreme. And then there was their inflation. At one point in the early twenties, the German mark became a joke. People used their currency as wallpaper—literally—it wasn't worth the paper it was printed on. The mark—which had once been as substantial to them as the dollar. So, yes, almost everything had gone absolutely wrong in Germany, and to top it you had a weak liberal government that wasn't even liberal. There's no comparison to present-day America. If fascism does come here, it will approach slowly. The one thing we can count on is it won't be called fascism and there won't be party men in uniform. If it is a hundred miles from here to Hitler, we've gone one mile so far. Every time someone on the left opens their mouth and says, "This is like Hitler," they are just encouraging their own people to grow more stupid. The one thing the Left has got to do, if it is not to become even more intellectually anemic (a.k.a. politically correct) is to keep some balance in its critical spirit.

JBM: So you see no similarities between what was going on with Germany and the condition in America now?

NM: If worst came to worst, we would have a totally different kind of fascism. Recognize that Nazi Germany was indeed the worst of all. The Italians had Mussolini, but his fascism wasn't nearly so bad as the German variety. Cruelty in those Italian years was not one part in ten, maybe not one part in a hundred of the comparable viciousness in Nazi Germany. Hitlerism was a thing unto itself, never seen before or since. To start comparing every last little thing here to Nazi Germany is to fortify the self-righteousness of the worst Republicans. The purpose of the Right in America is to keep the majority here as stupid as possible. Then they can run the country with less mass opposition. The Left does not help itself if it looks to share that stupidity. My argument with Michael Moore, for all the good he did, is that *Fahrenheit 9/11* also activates time-worn clichés and old stupidities on the left.

Terrorism

JBM: If the administration had to intensify the paranoia we were all feeling about terrorism to sell the war in Iraq, how much of our fear is legitimate? In other words, how scared should we be of terrorism?

NM: We're too afraid. And I hope I don't have to eat my words. But I do assume that at present, these terrorists are doing their utmost, and what they can do is not necessarily all that much, not against the huge forces being set in place against them.

Now, this may sound cold-blooded, but I think we overreact in our fear, and the reason is our bad conscience. Bad

conscience is running through America like a runaway
river.

There were 3,000 men and women killed on 9/11. That
number has been used over and over again. No one ever talks
anymore about the almost 60,000 Americans who were killed
in Vietnam, or the 400,000 of our soldiers killed in the Second
World War, or the 110,000 killed in the First World War. We
don't even know the numbers. We don't care. But these 3,000
are etched into our history. It's as if a giant hand picked up
America and tore it from its roots. We've been terror-stricken
ever since. Yet, we feel no terror that every year 40,000 people
get killed here in automobile accidents. We don't carry on
about that. Why? Because the car is absolutely necessary to us.
So I'd say civilized society itself is also necessary to us, and if we
end up with some large number, relatively, of people being
killed by terrorists every year, well, look at Israel. They're a
functioning country. They pay a heavy price to terrorism, but
it's not a final price.

JBM: Yes, but one major difference between car accidents and
terrorism is that with a car accident, no one intentionally set
out to take the life of your loved ones.

NM: For the families of the victims of car crashes, the emotional cost is analogous. It all seems so abrupt, so irrational, and—the root of it—so divinely heartless.

All the same, our fear of terrorism occupies center stage. It succeeds in numbing a larger and more important question, which is: What do we want of this country, and where do we wish to go? It may be that we would do well to recognize (and this will be an odious remark to a great many Americans) that the apex of our power has passed. We are now a very powerful nation in a world of three or four other very powerful nations. If we could make our peace with that, my guess is that terrorist acts against us might diminish. Because one aspect of present terrorism is the reaction to our arrogance. Muslims, living for generations in a culture tricked and defeated (or so they feel) by the progress of history, have to loathe the arrogance of that country which has profited the most by history in the last two centuries.

Environment, Profit, and Karma

JBM: Bush has two daughters whom, it seems, he genuinely loves and cares about. Yet his total lack of interest in the environment —his sluggishness in pursuing alternative sources of energy— signifies to me that the coming generations are of little concern to him. Do you think Bush cares about the future?

NM: Well, I don't know. I don't want to make fun of what you're saying, but that strikes me as—what can I say?—watery liberalism. I suppose Bush assumes he cares tremendously about the future. After all, he believes God speaks to him every night. He takes himself seriously. How often is there a president of a large country who doesn't take himself seriously? The question becomes: Is the way in which he takes himself seriously good and responsible, or is it asinine? I would choose the latter. As a president, Bush has attained the highest level of asininity. But that doesn't mean he can't take himself seriously, or not care about his daughters and think, "Oh, I've got to protect life for them." Of course he does. It's just his idea of how to proceed is different from the way you see it because he doesn't think about environmentalism as you do. He's talking to high corporate figures who say to him, "Listen, between us, there's nothing to worry about. Those liberals are just piping away on tin whistles. The environment is safe."

JBM: I can't imagine that's what they truly believe. I think it's more, "Yeah, the environment is a problem, but what it would cost to clean up our act could send us into an economic tailspin, and that's more of a problem than the temperature rising a few degrees over the next fifty years."

NM: That's true to a degree, but then again they are not going to lose their profits so quickly. Already, they must be looking ahead at how to stay on top of the wave if the environment turns sour—looking for protective programs they will come forward with (whether they work or not). You're going at it too directly. You're not old enough yet to know how various and creative are the self-exculpations in the mentality of the prosperous. They find more ways to forgive what they're doing than you take account of.

JBM: I suppose. I'm just thinking of self-preservation from their point of view.

NM: They would look upon you as being Desperate Ambrose.

JBM: Desperate Ambrose?

NM: You're seeing disaster immediately upon us. All they feel is that this is what liberals would like to believe because they're out of power.

JBM: What I'm seeing is if we don't start implementing changes now, when we reach the point where we *have* to, it's going to be too late.

NM: A great many environmentalists have been saying this for twenty years. They're right or they're wrong—I don't know.

But recognize that people in any administration, no matter how intelligent or capable, do not work all that rationally. They work instead for their self-serving interests.

That is the way they got there. Rarely will you have a change of heart at the top. One or another may come to a deeper recognition of the real needs of humanity and society, but that's unusual. Most often, they're quite happy with the way they got there. Because they succeeded, they feel reinforced by their own previous career actions. So, they're not about to change in a hurry. And they do laugh at us. Argument is not going to move them. They laugh at our arguments.

JBM: Sad laughter.

NM: No, their laugh is hearty. Our laughter is sad.

JBM: Not if one believes in Karma.

NM: All right, Karma. You want to get into Karma?

JBM: How long can you take your profit at the expense of the vast majority and not have it come back to haunt you?

NM: Well, so long as the devil—now we're getting into something else—so long as the devil is able to work with a command of power comparable to God, Karma must also be fucked-up. If God does not control Karma altogether, if the devil has his input into Karma as well, then these guys at the top can prosper for a long time. They can say, "I'm an evil man, and I'll be reborn as an evil man."

JBM: (*Laughs*)

NM: "Yes," they say, "I like it, I like it. And I go to church every Sunday—you can count on that." I expect that is how they think, John.

PART TWO

Courage, Morality, and Sexual Pleasure*

PLAYBOY: *"I did it because I could." Thus explains President Clinton on his motive for his affair with Monica Lewinsky. This would appear to be the motive for much of Boomerdom. "I did drugs because I could." "I had sex because I could." It is not so much immorality as amorality that drives such behavior. In the absence of moral order or authority, the fool is free to pursue all courses with abandon. Is amorality more troublesome than immorality?*

NM: Immorality is a clearer concept. We know we're up to

---

* The following first appeared in *Playboy*, December 2004.

something that by our moral logic is forbidden. "Amoral" is more ambiguous. It falls into several categories. People can be amoral in business, or in their loyalties, but generally speaking, we think of an amoral man as a sexist. Even that word has its subcategories. One type doesn't give a damn about the partner. His pleasure goes into achievement. Such a dude will measure prowess by how many times he gets laid. Even more important: What rating did the woman give him?

Then there's biological amorality. The man is suffering a heavy physical need. The need is more important to him than the partner. That's animal, if you will, but it is not as related to the ego.

JBM: Can there ever truly be amorality? For me, everybody, whether they know it or not, lives by a code, and when they break their own code, it bothers them.

NM: Okay, some amoral people do work by a code. That's more interesting. Let's say that for them the whole moral system is a lot of crap. So, ignore it. They believe that any orthodox moral system breeds illness, pain, frustration, and deception of oneself. The old *Playboy* philosophy used to weigh in on how we have to change our sexual mores. "Stick to one woman" was not what Hef was all about.

I would say this aspect of amorality can be justified. One can argue that we have the right to make many sorties into sex when we are single, and to find new partners all the time. The underlying notion is that sooner or later, the cumulative knowledge we gain will ready us for a serious love. Many a sexist who has a rep as a good lover might, under all that, be dreaming of a great love to come. Such studs are getting ready for the big meeting by having many affairs en route to the championship. More than one movie star subscribes to this psychology. Seen as a vehicle to increase one's knowledge, amorality becomes more interesting.

Henry Miller once said something to the effect that there's no such thing as a bad fuck. I think he meant that no matter how horrible it can get, you always learn something about the woman and about yourself. Some people do dig into fucking like gold miners. They're not worrying about the earth—they want the goddamn gold. If the pickax strikes rock, they'll go elsewhere.

JBM: Do you learn more from sleeping with ten women, or sleeping with one woman for ten years?

NM: A man full of sensuality would probably opt for the first course. You need to feel extraordinary love to be faithful to someone for ten years. After my own checkered career, being married six times, with eight children and one terrific stepson—I've been on both sides of that question.

I've certainly been amoral in my day. Cold as ice with a few. But on the other hand, I've been attracted immensely to the qualities that women have. My amorality—if we're going to get into it—was a search. I wanted to learn more about sex. I sometimes think if pornography had come along when I was a young man, it would have dispensed with a lot of friction in my personal life. Because you do learn a lot from pornography. Women's animal qualities are exemplified positively or negatively in a porny film. Besides, you might be a little less likely to marry the first woman you find who is highly sexual.

JBM: I want to get back to Clinton's quote: "I did it because I could." What are your thoughts on the way he referred to Monica Lewinsky in his book?

NM: As people go, Clinton is not the worst guy you're going to meet. He has a lot of natural warmth, plus a good deal of everything else a president needs: calculation, manipulation, interest in his work, all of that. In this case, I thought his particular remarks were needlessly cruel. I believe he would have preferred to speak nicely about Monica Lewinsky, but you've got to remember he has an angry and injured wife on his hands. He had to weigh in with something to satisfy her—Hillary was more on his mind than Monica.

"I did it because I could" is an empty remark. Anyone who's met Monica knows she's very attractive. She's got beautiful coloring, she's intense, she's bright—that's the real reason why he did it.

And for another reason entirely, which may be richer, although it is certainly meaner. A most intelligent woman I know once said, "Clinton lived in a minimum-security prison. Every fifteen minutes, security checked up on where he was." I thought, She's absolutely right. What we're dealing with here was an incarcerated man. It's as if he was in the finest, grandest minimum-security prison in the world, the White House. In that sense, 5 percent of him is a convict.

JBM: And once you're in prison, you do what you can get away with.

NM: Exactly.

JBM: Then his remark is not so hollow.

NM: I see what you're saying—yes, it's not as hollow as I thought. He did it not because he could, but because he wanted to get away with it. He could turn his incarceration a little bit around. Nonetheless, I still think the style of phrasing comes because of his wife. Having been married six times, I have some idea of what one says on such occasions.

JBM: You're a good one to talk to about that. But, more to the point, Bill Clinton has a wife who plans to run for high office. Is it immoral or amoral to make a calculated decision to strip humanity away from Monica in order to protect the image of his wife as a strong potential candidate?

NM: Both. Immoral in that he is most calculatedly not telling the truth about his real feelings. It's amoral because he wants to keep the political process going: all politicians have to be amoral to a degree. It's a question of how much. Are they 44 percent amoral or 88 percent? Politicians cannot possibly afford morality except as a series of specious sentiments ready to be uttered as patriotic or theological slogans. A politician has to deal with the given. That means they can even tell the truth at times. Usually, they're only pretending. Politicians build up profound habits of not addressing the truth head-on. In practice, they have to shake hands with people they can't bear, and proffer patriotic remarks that don't come from the heart.

Now, whether immoral, amoral, or both, it was, finally, a necessity. It was—the two holy words for politicians—*the given.*

JBM: Isn't it possible for a politician to live by his own code today?

NM: No. Not a successful politician.

JBM: Was it possible in FDR's day?

NM: It's never possible. Go back to the maxim: "Politics is the art of the possible." What's important is to get some part of what you want done. That's how a democracy works. By pieces and parts.

The irony is, the only way you can come near a direct expression of your personality is in a dictatorship. Of course, as democrats, we feel instinctively that no human being is good enough to be entrusted with that kind of power. So in a democracy, change always comes from negotiation. When adversaries walk away from a political compact, each side is a bit dissatisfied.

JBM: I'm still too much of an optimist. I think that's choice B.

NM: Well, if you ever get into politics, you're going to discover how many compromises have to be made, willy-nilly.

JBM: I suppose that's true. In the end, the distinguishing factor between a decent politician and a corporate puppet is not *if* he is willing to compromise, but *what* he is willing to compromise.

PLAYBOY: *You've written about the cultural necessity of literature. Yet we now live in a time when the novelist and literature itself are borderline irrelevant. There's an absence of interiority, of serious, concentrated thought. We may be in danger of losing literature forever. What would this mean for American culture?*

NM: As a novelist, I'm now speaking from my vested position. My profession is being eroded. When I began, good novelists were more important in the scheme of things. The irony is that the great novelists like Hemingway and Faulkner probably didn't sell as many copies per book as a few serious novelists sell now. But they were revered. They affected history. They had their impact on America. Hemingway was a prodigious influence for young American writers. He taught a lot of us how to look for the tensile strength of a sentence.

I think a nation's greatness depends, to a real extent, on

how well-spoken its citizens are. Good things develop out of a populace that really knows how to use the language and use it well. Would Great Britain have been able to manage the empire in the nineteenth century without their three hundred and more years of reading Shakespeare? Where would Ireland be today without Joyce? Not as prosperous, I expect. As a language deteriorates, becomes less eloquent, less metaphorical, less salient, less poignant, a curious deadening of the human spirit comes seeping in.

By now, America has shifted from being a country with a great love of freedom and creativity (in constant altercation with those other Americans who wanted rule and order) into a country that's now much more interested in power. And power, I can promise you, is not interested in metaphor. Metaphor is antagonistic to power because it pushes you to think in more poetic and contradictory ways. Power demands a unilinear approach. Power does not welcome poetic concepts.

JBM: But hasn't power always been a driving force in society?

NM: Always. But it was situated among other driving forces such as culture and art and love of sports and good architecture and tradition. Now it's as if corporate power has become the most dominant theme of our lives. In ten more years, you won't find a professional stadium that is not named for a corporation.

JBM: Or a Broadway theater. The lack of rage against that from the artistic community is depressing but not surprising. The majority of the biggest celebrities today are manufactured by the largest corporations. It's hardly in their interest to bite the hand that feeds them, even if that hand is turning the name of a theater into an advertisement for the company. Gone are the days when writers had the same influence as rock stars. Justin Timberlake, who I'm sure is a nice guy, nonetheless should not be one of the people influencing a generation. He's a pop singer. His career was created by Disney. Part of his job is not to have an opinion. Somewhere between the lines, I'm not sure where, it shifted from great minds speaking to the masses to celebrities speaking to the masses.

NM: Be careful. You're too young to know how it was back then. Great minds almost never speak directly to the masses.

JBM: Not directly. But Hemingway would write a piece, you would write a piece, and people would discuss it and debate it, go back and forth—

NM: Leave me out of it.

JBM: To this day, people who read *The White Negro* when they were teenagers come up to me and want to argue about it. It still affects them nearly fifty years later. I don't think any essay written by anyone today could do the same. There are too many other forms of media that are digested more easily, too easily.

NM: Why not use a rating system for ideas? The most profound ideas are those one is willing to die for. By that measure, Karl Marx has to be one of the greatest writers who ever lived. Because hundreds of thousands of people in his time and after were willing to die for his ideas. All over the world, millions were willing to go to prison for them. This is not to raise a latter-day defense of Marx. He had incredible virtues as a thinker. From my point of view, he also had his lacks. He certainly didn't understand that atheism is not a way to win the world. You can't. Not by that route. Half the people alive—or is it three-quarters?—have instinctive notions that God exists. I think the real failure of Bolshevism, then Stalinism, was clinging to the idea that religion is the opium of the masses. Organized religion may well be its own species of narcotic, but the concept that we are part of divine Creation is something else altogether.

If we're ever going to have a great society in the future—which is hardly a guaranteed conclusion—if we ever build a world with real freedom, we may have to arrive at the recognition that we can dispense with fundamentalism, and live instead with the idea that God is a Creator, not a lawgiver.

JBM: To shift the subject back to your home turf, who is going to be the last serious novelist?

NM: Probably someone analogous to the poor poet today who is writing five-act verse plays in iambic pentameter. I do foresee a day when very few will look at serious fiction. Instead, they will read computer novels. The computer is better suited to turn out a best seller than a mediocre novelist. But not too many people will still be interested in serious literary work. Whole populations will be looking for technological power rather than exploring those moral questions they hope to ponder anywhere but in the serious novel.

The best fiction has always been the seedbed for the most interesting and subtle moral questions, questions that, at best, go deeper than the wisdom you can receive in any church or synagogue or mosque. When it comes to moral paradox, theology is limited. It's too structured. Interesting morality almost never fits prearranged moral codes. It's only the novelist—the very good novelist—who can deal with such moral issues as "Am I *on balance* a good person or a bad one?" You don't find that out by declaring, "Well, I'm good because I obey the Ten Commandments." That doesn't make you good. You can still be a horror if you restrict the lives of others with your piety. The real question is, How do you affect other people's lives? The best novels are marvelous for delving into the subtler questions of our nature.

After all, what is human nature? We're still finding that out. It is immensely various, even as God, I believe, is immensely various. We're the children, if you will, of the Creator. I believe that God doesn't want to give us orders from above; rather, He wishes us to discover things about our nature that we can send back to Him. Or Her. Does the parent always wish to be superior to the child? No. Most parents want their children to surpass them.

JBM: One would hope that very reason, right there, is enough to keep the novel alive.

NM: You're leaving out the social imperatives of the people who run things. An immensely powerful global capitalism is shaping up. That capitalism does not need or look for inquiry into delicate matters. Its need, rather, is to keep the bullshit train running at top speed. It has to enforce the self-serving notion that corporations are good for human existence. It needs to have most people believing that big business is the only way to do it. The last thing those gentlemen need is novels.

Part of the genius of corporate capitalism is that they've found ways to control people that are so much subtler than the old Stalinist procedures. Those methods were brutal, dull, cold, stupid, and openly oppressive. The modern form of oppression is nuanced; it gets into your psyche—it makes you think there's something wrong with you if you're not on the big capitalist team. So they don't want writers exploring into morality. They want one morality, theirs. Unlike Stalinism at its worst, it's more of a benign regime, superficially open and ready for the development of technology which will make all our lives extraordinary—sure, technology will end up keeping us alive for 150 or 200 years, even if three-quarters of each of us will be replacement parts. "I'm on my fourth heart," says the man who is 200 years old. I'm not sure that's either God's intention or the real human intention. It may be an ultimate destruction of the human spirit to stay alive beyond a certain point. Maybe death is as important to life as life itself. To keep extending the years of your life—that could be one more form of evil. Much too much is being taken for granted today.

But I must go back to the original point: the good novel, the serious novel, is antipathetic to corporate capitalism. The best seller is one of the props of corporate capitalism precisely because it's an entertainment. "At the end of the day, I want to have fun," says the nine-to-fiver. "Give me asshole TV shows, exploitation films with lots of bang. I don't need to read a good book—I want a page-turner." Well, every time there's a page-turner to read for too little, someone's mind is being dulled. Even page-turners can get into interesting questions, but dependably, they will always veer away from moral exploration.

JBM: I think the challenge is to make a serious novel entertaining so people can't put it down. That's the only way to compete with the various other forms of media.

NM: I started as that kind of writer, and I know how easy it is. It's routine to write a page-turner. There are such simple rules. I can teach any mediocre writer to turn one out. But I'm interested in something that's good enough and well enough written so that you have to stop on the page and read a sentence over a few times. Why? Because it vibrates within you. A page-turner is equal to a fast-paced sitcom.

JBM: What are your thoughts on the power that Oprah Winfrey wields over a book? You know, recently she put *Anna Karenina* on her Book of the Month list and it became a best seller again.

NM: I salute her for that. It so happens *Anna Karenina* is one of my all-time favorite novels. I had that and *War and Peace* on my desk while I was writing *The Naked and the Dead.* To get steamed up to write every morning, I'd read five or ten pages of *Anna Karenina.* So, yes, I applaud her for that.

JBM: Because she has such popular mass appeal, she can take something that is hard to read and make it a best seller. That gives me hope.

NM: But if she keeps doing it, her popularity will begin to diminish and then we'll begin to see the real test of her character. Is she devoted to great literature or is she, quite naturally, a little more devoted to the power of her own career?

JBM: Perhaps through the power of her own career, she can raise great literature back to the popular level of best sellers.

NM: No. No person can do that. You're so young you still believe in the power of individuals. The hard fact—which I would like to see develop in you, my friend, over the next ten years, is a much deeper sense of social structure. Because society is paramount. It's as if we're little animals running through the machine. Occasionally we touch a switch, something starts, we start another little machine, but we can't really alter the nature of the machine that much. Not without great study and long-term devotion plus willingness to get into the grease of the gears.

JBM: And great luck. No, I respect the complexity of the social machine—I don't think one person can change it by themselves, but I do agree with Robert F. Kennedy that every action you take is equivalent to throwing a pebble into a pond. It's the ripples that affect the machine.

NM: The ripples die out.

JBM: But they can go pretty far if they're strong enough.

NM: How many times does a pebble thrown into a pond change the nature of the shoreline? Let's stop the crap.

PLAYBOY: *Provincetown in midwinter. How is it to live in a place that seems abandoned and bereft? Is it better than during the high season?*

NM: For a writer of my age, it's better in the off-season. There's an old saying about P'town that in the winter you can roll a bowling ball down Commercial Street and it'll never hit anyone. So it is lonely here in February and March and mean and cold. It's damp, it's lonely, and I love it. It fits my mood. It's much easier to spend the day writing if it's gray outside. Besides, the people I used to know here years ago are dead now. (Most of them from drink.) Provincetown has changed profoundly since. In summer, it's now the gay capital of the Northeast. Forty or fifty years ago, it used to be the Wild West of the East—you had motorcycle gangs coming in on Saturdays. And at 1 a.m. on Sunday morning, you'd have people going up in the hills for bacchanals, everybody carrying booze or beer. Marriages broke up and serious affairs started on many of those nights.

JBM: Well, you still have motorcycle gangs coming in—it's just that now they're wearing helmets, sunglasses, leather chaps, and nothing else.

NM: *(laughs)* All right.

JBM: Having spent a lot of time in Provincetown growing up, I don't think of it as a gay town. As a member of the heterosexual underground, I see it as a very libertarian place. As long as you're not hurting anyone else, whatever you're doing is cool. And, because there is so much sexual energy flying through the air, the hetero nightlife is jumping.

NM: Good to hear that. There's always been so much going on in Provincetown. There are amazing contradictions here. After all, this is the place where the Pilgrims first landed.

JBM: Why did they leave?

NM: Like all good white people who are righteous and not quite aware of how mean they can be underneath their righteousness, they were full of themselves. After all, they had dared to leave their roots and sail across the Atlantic cramped in a small boat. They got here through true difficulty. At the end, it was even hard to navigate the waters around Cape Cod, but there is a natural harbor in Provincetown where the land curls around in a spiral. So they made anchor in this harbor—parenthetically, the spot where they rowed their longboat to land now offers a huge motel. We are nothing in America if not highly adaptive to profit. The Puritans, however, found the soil not particularly welcoming, full of sand, brush pine, low country, not good for farming. They were in search of food, went scouting around. While reconnoitering eight miles south of Provincetown, they found a place in Truro (now called Corn Hill) where the Indians had stored their grain for the coming winter. So the Puritans brought the corn back to their ship, and in the reverberations of that action may have killed a couple of redskins. There is argument about this last point. In any event, shortly after, one of those Puritans probably said to another, "Prithee, brother, let's get the fuck out." So they sailed to the other side of Massachusetts Bay, some forty miles across the water, and moved into Plymouth, which then became the founding place of America. Hail to the first Thanksgiving.

Well, a couple of hundred years later, the locals here became furious at the ongoing self-serving pride of Plymouth. How did that town dare to call itself the founding place of America? So they started petitioning Washington, D.C. By 1909, that got so hot that a beautiful tower was erected through subscriptions, a copy of an Italian tower in Siena, and Theodore Roosevelt actually came to the opening festivities here. This exceptionally phallic tower is now called the Pilgrim Monument.

JBM: So America started with white people stealing corn, killing natives, and going on the lam?

NM: Yes.

PLAYBOY: *Did women's sexuality shape human evolution? According to a theory in Leonard Shlain's new book,* Sex, Time and Power, *menstruation is what enabled women to develop a sense of time and forethought. Language evolved, he says, primarily because men and women had to negotiate sex. Women became expert at reading between the lines of various Pleistocenes. Beauty was developed to maintain the interest of men. Is this why women control men?*

NM: I haven't read the book, but that theory does strike me as wobbly. For example, negotiating sex. Where is the new idea there? After all, even animals negotiate sex. I had two standard poodles once, many years ago, Tibo and Zsa-Zsa, and Zsa-Zsa was one hell of a bitch, always nipping at Tibo's nuts. I was afraid Tibo would end up as no man at all by the time he came of age—we first had them when they were pups. How she dominated him—she had fierce teeth. He'd have to duck, and sit down fast. These earlier negotiations had taught him a lot, however. He knew what was called for. When Zsa-Zsa came into heat for the first time, he seized her with hardly a by-your-leave and impregnated her. Nine pups for one round. Before they were done, they created thirty-four new standard poodles over the next three years. An ongoing negotiation. Animals not only have a great deal of language in their grunts, their groans, their whines, their moans, their baying at the moon, but their *scents*. Odor used to have more to do with sex than language—at least until deodorants came on the scene. But before the advent of whiff-deadening products in spray cans, any combination of strong genital odor mixed with perfume was pretty damned aphrodisiacal, yessir, all through every barnyard and royal court of Europe right through the Second World War. So the notion that language had to be developed to facilitate sex cannot, by my lights, have merit.

JBM: What about a sense of time developed through menstruation?

NM: There I see a point. Menstruation certainly proved to women that they were altogether different from men. So, they had to have a different code.

JBM: This other question—do women control men? For one, do you think so?

NM: Completely.

JBM: I'm glad you agree.

NM: Before women's liberation came along, men used to have some purchase on control in a marriage. Perhaps 35 percent. The woman had the remaining 65. Now, after women's liberation, it's up to 95 percent.

JBM: Wow . . .

NM: I could be wrong. Maybe it's only 85 percent.

JBM: Is this why men are forever at a loss in regard to the dominance of women?

NM: Well, women are closer to the universe. Closer to creation than we are. So, they have deeper instincts.

JBM: They create life, we destroy life.

NM: Oh, let's not get into that. Women have deadened as many men in subtle ways, for subtle reasons, as men have beaten women down in more overt fashion.

JBM: I'm not saying one is more vicious than the other. I'm saying, traditionally, men have gone to war and women have raised the children. That's changing. Women are going to war and we've seen what happens at Abu Ghraib.

NM: Yes, that poor pregnant girl . . .

JBM: I feel for her—I do.

NM: You do?

JBM: She was in the wrong place with the wrong guys, feeling the wrong pressures, and now she's all alone.

NM: She really is. I also can see how wild the parties are getting all over America this season. The key factor at Abu Ghraib was, "Hey, none of you at home are going to believe this until you see our pictures." And the photograph taking that was not called for by their superiors—as well as the photos that were— after all, some of the photos were used to blackmail the prisoners into talking. "You don't want your family to see this," was overtly behind a lot of that. But the Abu Ghraib gang were also delighted to send these photos home to their friends. Just think of the kind of party that's been going on back in America while Bush keeps talking about how splendid a Christian nation we are.

You know, I love this country with all its faults, but one of its huge spiritual crimes is that we're the bullshit kingdom of all time. We've found a way to process bullshit so you can't even smell the bull any longer.

JBM: What do you think of the gender roles of men and women now that women are expected to raise a family *and* be successful in the workplace?

NM: For me, any notion that males are superior to females or females superior to males is, I'd say, like comparing dogs to cats. To my mind, it's a hopeless argument. Men are so fundamentally different from women.

I still have to say that the desire for power in women that's revealed itself in the last thirty-five years is not attractive. The power they used to have was vastly more attractive. It used to be fun to realize a woman was smarter than you. In the course of living one's life and learning how to handle oneself, there were women who developed such tasty subtleties about how to control us. They were like animal handlers, if you will. And the animal, even the lion, almost always adores the handler. Now they're dominating us openly: "The whip and the knout for you, buddy, we are the politically correct."

JBM: I don't think I agree with that. It's changing. There was the height of political correctness in the mid to late nineties that was terrifying. But the majority of women I know today want a real man—they don't want a man they can walk all over.

NM: Well, good. I'm eighty-two, and these unhappy experiences occurred to me thirty years ago.

JBM: You were living then at the height of the gender war. But what's truly encouraging, what's encouraging me now, is I see more women in power positions, but women who do it the way a woman does it, not the way a man would do it if he were a woman.

NM: Name a few, would you?

JBM: Arianna Huffington, Laura Dawn of MoveOn.org, Hillary Clinton—

NM: Hillary Clinton is a very good example. I met her many years ago when she was the governor's wife in Arkansas. Probably in '84. She was immensely intelligent—I happened to sit next to her at dinner—and we had a very good conversation. I was impressed with how bright she was, how open, and what a fine mind she had. She's not as interesting now. Today, she's a politician. She's very cautious. Her books are boring. What's that one, *It Takes a Village* . . . full of cant. The way Maggie Thatcher was full of cant. You say what's useful to say, not what you believe. You never speak from the heart. Hillary is always watch-dogging her tongue these days. Totally unspontaneous in exactly the way an average mediocre-to-good, effective politician oversees his spiel.

JBM: But as we said before, she's a politician at a high level— she has no choice.

NM: So why get excited about her as a role model?

JBM: I'm not saying we're there yet. But I do see people coming up in the ranks. I see Laura Dawn helping to open up politics to the people. I see Arianna Huffington approaching political media from a new angle and having a surprising amount of success in terms of her ability to frame the argument. Politics this year has been more exciting than ever before, in my lifetime certainly. It's sexier, it's getting to be more fun.

NM: All right. I can see a time when women are more important politically than they are now, and for better reasons, but that doesn't mean anything much is going to change. In a certain sense, a politician, regardless of gender, is neutered by the process. A lot of politicians are attractive in person because, after all, they're pressing the flesh. All the time. Shake a thousand hands in a morning and an afternoon and you're horny by the end of the day. The hands are telling you something. Where's the guy who won't get a hard-on if he's admired by a lot of women? But, nonetheless, politics dehumanizes you. I don't say this out of sour grapes because when I ran for mayor in that Democratic primary back in 1969, I considered it my duty. Believe it or not, I felt God wanted me to go into politics to save New York. I was a high-octane fool. And I wasn't nearly as good as I thought I'd be. All the same, I was prepared to pay the price. I knew I would never write again in any serious way if I got elected. I knew I would use up my soul then in ways that were unhappy for me. But I felt: "I haven't been a good guy—I want to save my soul." Now, this was not only simplistic thinking (which is no drawback to running for high office), but I turned out to be an ineffectual politician. All the same, I was ready to bite the bullet. What I learned from the effort and the defeat is that politics is a tremendously difficult business. You know, we respect basketball players because they have such stamina. Well, very few humans can become good politicians due to the amount of work you run into. The responsibilities. The number of distasteful things you have to do. So I don't sneer at politicians. I think they're entitled to the same kind of respect we give reasonably good athletes. Stamina is impressive. But I don't have any illusion that in becoming a politician you become a nobler person—very rarely does that occur. The only reason it happens once in a while is because it's an impossible Creation if you can't have exceptions to every last rule.

PLAYBOY: *You once wrote somewhere: "As many people die from an excess of timidity as from bravery. Nobody ever mentions that." Do you care to give an explanation of courage?*

NM: I have one. It's ready-made. Courage can only be measured by the place from which you start. Picture an old lady who is ill in every joint, terribly arthritic, nonetheless she has to cross a difficult street and she can't quite keep up with the lights. Nonetheless she feels an inner imperative to move. And she does manage to get across, even though she's terrified. I would call that courage. I would say it is analogous to the case of a well-trained Marine, a good kid, who gets into combat, sees his buddies wounded, sees a good friend killed, goes through hell. He gets to the point where he expects he will die. Until that moment, you can't really speak of his courage. He's been trained to be brave—you can motivate people to be brave. But when you get to that crux in combat where you say, "It's not worth it. I'm scared shitless, I can't go on, I want to quit, I don't care about my buddies, fuck it all, I want to quit"—and then another side of you takes over and says, "You *will* go on, whether you die or not, you will go on"—that's courage.

Otherwise, courage can be meaningless. If you're in a very easy war, and very well trained in your martial skills, you may feel panic, but you're prepared to be brave.

So, I would say, courage is transcendence. Whatever our level of competence at more or less hairy activities, we are still obliged to go beyond ourselves, to transcend ourselves, if we wish to rise so high as courage itself.

That's why I say timidity kills. Kills more people than bravery because every time one's timid, one's pulling back creative impulses in oneself, denying them. One is denting one's ego. And as an ego contracts out of shame, illness begins. This is my opinion.

JBM: So is courage a virtue?

NM: Absolutely a virtue—Make it *the* virtue. I would go so far as to say that it's very hard to feel love if you're full of shame. We can only feel love for someone else when we have gained respect for ourselves—it's why we have this endless obsession with courage. Where is the man who can ignore it? It's analogous to a woman who will wear no makeup, no jewelry, won't comb her hair because she hates women who are elegant, feels those women are phony. "I want to be seen as my natural self." Yet that woman can never sneer at elegance with full confidence. A part of her feels there's something wrong with her. She doesn't want to get the utmost out of herself. By the same token, some men sneer at bravery, call it overrated, are always ready to point out how much trouble it breeds. Of course it does. A macho brute is a macho brute. But not even a saint can sneer at bravery with a completely clear and open heart. Not even a saint.

JBM: You know, one of the outcomes of living in such an organized society where everything is taken care of—men don't go out, kill their food, and bring it back, etc.—is there's a complicity, almost a sense of deliberately forgetting that when you get right down to it, ultimately we're animals. We will fight each other down to our last bite when our own is attacked. And I don't know if this is true of everybody, but 95 percent of the time when I meet another man, under it all is that sense of "Could I take you or could you take me?" And it's usually a kind of fun, but it's always there. Something like 9/11 reminds us all, on a national level, that tomorrow, like that *(snaps fingers)*, most of our societal luxuries could be gone and we're back to grunting and biting. That's important. I think it's one of the major differences between the mentality of a man in the new millennium and the mentality of a man in the nineties, when political correctness was at its height and the sensitive ponytailed guy was getting laid more than he should.

NM: Well, I think you have an unbalanced situation when the sensitive—or oversensitive—ponytailed guy is getting laid more than the macho brute.

JBM: I don't know that he was getting laid more. He was just getting laid more than he should. And for too little.

NM: Oh, you're a bigot.

JBM: I've got my prejudices.

NM: Yes, you may have received them from your father.

PLAYBOY: *In Freud's essay, "The Uncanny," he contends that the strongest instances of the uncanny involve "doubts whether an apparently animate being is really alive, or conversely, whether a lifeless object might not be in fact animate." We live in an age where such distinctions become even less clear. This is indeed frightening. We're overmatched by our technology. Our ability to comprehend is exceeded by the ability to construct and fabricate. You have spoken of the inanimate—that which cannot be animated. Increasingly, it seems, we are overcome by this uncanniness. Is there more of this to come in our future?*

NM: I say absolutely yes. So long as technology expands and expands, we're going to have more of such uneasiness. I remember back in '69, I was down at NASA, south of Houston, covering the first landing on the moon, the flight of Apollo 11.

In the book I wrote about it, there was a chapter called "The Psychology of Machines," which discussed the immense amount of attention these NASA technicians gave to glitches. It truly worried the venture—there was something so spooky about glitches. NASA had the best technology available, and yet the most inexplicable little malfunctions would occur. It obsessed them. The real question, I decided (even though they would never admit it to themselves), was "Do machines have a psychology?" Do things go wrong because machines have temperaments?

JBM: Are we talking about a psychology or a soul?

NM: You're beyond me on that one. I was asking if there was an inner life in the machine that we were not in touch with. You rarely find a person now who has a computer who doesn't feel their little magic box has a personality. Or cars—everyone feels that his car has its own presence. Of course, this last is a case where the uncanny doesn't scare us, it pleases us almost.

JBM: You know, whenever I hook my computer up to the Internet, she reacts very poorly. A number of other people I know had the same experience I think it's because plugging the Internet into your computer is the equivalent of 10,000 phalli being inserted out of the blue. She's saying, "Hey, I just want yours. What is this?"

NM: I think Freud put his finger on the nature of the uncanny. Part of what is so depressing about modern technology is the way it cuts off our senses. One of the things most awful about plastic—and I've been fulminating against plastic—most unsuccessfully—for the last thirty, forty years—is that plastic is *not* uncanny. It's just there, inert. It's very hard to conceive of any kind of soul or spirit inhabiting the stuff because it doesn't come out of nature but from a set of factory processes. Even a wooden cane has a touch of personality, but plastic doesn't. I've always felt it is the handmaiden to technology. Why do people love technology? It gives you more power than you'd have without the technology, but you pay a heavy price. You become a little more inert in your finer sensibilities.

JBM: Where is our technology leading us? A car is certainly a piece of technology, but not until recently was there plastic all over it.

NM: Yes, as they make plastic stronger, and more analogous to steel—which they will—so, in turn, cars are going to be made entirely of plastic because economically speaking, the plastic substitute offers more profit. No surprise then if the mediocrities have taken over the world under the banner of technology, corporate vision, and the unholy urge to purvey democracy to all countries of the world, whether they're ready for it, or capable of it. But we tell them, in effect, "You are going to end up a democracy whether you want it or not." This turns democracy into a farce. Because democracy is a grace. Any true democracy is sensitive enough to be perishable, and we're in danger right now of losing our democracy right here. The people who are running the world at present, very badly in many places, have the feeling that successfully controlled direction is the only answer. My feeling, of course, is exactly the opposite. Global capitalism does not speak of a free market but of a controlled globe. It is alien to the creative possibilities that have not yet been tapped in legions of people who've never had a chance to be creative, who work and die without creative moments in their lives. But their hopes, I believe, have been buried in their gene stream for generations, and are passed on. When talented people emerge from no apparent cultural background, I see them as the product of these ten generations of frustration from people who wanted to be more than their lives gave them. Such an artist is now receiving the bounty that was packed into the dreams of his or her forebears. This premise also works in reverse. Restrained evils, withheld evils, extended over many generations can end by producing a monster of a dictator.

JBM: There's an argument that our technology is stunting our evolution. Were we not spending so much time going out into the computer, focusing on TV, what have you, more people would have evolved to a higher psychic level. Instead, we're developing a technology where we have one device that will be your phone and your e-mail, your this, your that, your Internet access, a little device you carry with you all the time, or perhaps it's implanted in your head, that you'll program your likes and dislikes into. It will send out a signal and as you pass a stranger on the street—say you both like to watch *Star Trek*—a little bell will go off on both of your devices, signaling to you that compatibility is near by. Why are we doing this?

NM: Because of a deep fear. We've lost the often crippling but nonetheless intense consolations of religion. Formal, organized religion introduced many perversities into our nature, but it also offered many poor people some hope—if you were a good enough person, you'd enter heaven. But religion also stood in the way of development of capitalism and technology, corporate capitalism. A man running a small business is living by his wits, but people enter corporations in order not to have to live by their instincts—or, most important—their fears. Only a few have to take responsibility. The corporation can be a relatively benign organization, but it is still subtly totalitarian. And this is spreading. People at the top want to control the world because they're in terror that otherwise we are going to blow it up. My feeling is if the corporations take over the world, it will indeed blow apart because technology could end by violating too much of human nature.

JBM: Hasn't technology taken over the world already?

NM: Not completely. Not completely. There are still corners and avenues, games and places.

JBM: There's an underground.

NM: That underground has to go a long way before I will take it seriously, and yet I am ready to drink to that idea.

How Rich Do You Need to Be?

JBM: You once argued that in a well-balanced society, no one needs more money than you, as one example, manage to make. And I agree. You've been able to enjoy a comfortable living for much of your life, and now at the age of eighty-two you will even be able to leave some to your nine children, et cetera. Maybe each year you earn ten or fifteen times what the average guy makes. But CEOs of megacorporations take in one hundred, even one thousand times more than the guy on the bottom. That's a ridiculous disparity. Nobody needs that much. Is this the kind of disparity between rich and poor that could bring about a French-style revolution in America? And would we, as a country, be better off if it did?

NM: Well, I must say, I find fault with the way you're phrasing this. You're being too large, too speculative. To begin with, the French Revolution occurred after a thousand years of wrath had been installed and reinstalled into the French genes. Revolutions that transform countries emerge from a huge inchoate wrath. Over the centuries, one generation after another sees its own hopes abused until hope is replaced by concentrations of fury. The Russian Revolution that came at the end of World War I can serve as the prime example. That repetitive set of hideous conditions has not afflicted the greater number of people here. There is not that kind of wrath here in America.

Now, should we fall into a terrible depression—and I won't pretend to argue that we will or we won't—but if there is a total economic collapse here—then the fact that the fat cats had made so much money would indeed become onerous. Even onerous in the extreme. That is still a stage or two away from a violent revolution.

JBM: After talking to Cheri Honkala (who runs KWRU.org, an international advocacy organization for the homeless), and seeing the rage that is brewing, the rage she has so far been able to keep peaceful, whenever in the future, I might have the opportunity to talk to a CEO, I will be able to tell him with all sincerity, "It's in your interest to help these people out, because they're simply not going to take it forever. You could reduce your income 10 percent and not really feel it, but bringing their life up 10 percent could make the difference of a roof over their head and three meals a day for their children. You would keep the pot from boiling over." There's just no excuse for there to be a homeless problem in America today.

NM: Well, if you ever talk to a CEO, he'll be polite, but in private he'll be laughing at you. He'll be thinking, "That's all very well, kiddo, and it could even be that you may have to worry about this down the road, but I won't. I'm fifty-five years old," thinks the CEO, "and I'm really enjoying my yacht, my airplane, my private golf instructor. You can just keep talking."

JBM: But their kids are going to have to worry about it.

NM: CEOs often don't worry about their kids because their kids usually don't speak to them. Not in any real way.

Political Correctness and Racism

JBM: You stirred up a little trouble last summer with the Michiko Kakutani joke you made to Douglas Brinkley in *Rolling Stone*. Now, by my estimate, that was a foolish thing to say. I'm no fan of hers, but it was inaccurate, even as a joke. However, when I read that, I saw the twinkle in your eye and the laughter that came with the remark. The joking nature of it, but—

NM: I don't want to get into it. It's old spew. Let's face it. I made a big mistake. The fact is, Kakutani is no kamikaze. They, at least, were brave, whereas she may not have the outdoor guts of a pissant. She never appears in public. I don't know anyone who's ever met her. She writes in what must be a secret and most guarded hole and does her best to destroy any number of good writers. In the last month she gave hideous reviews to Michael Cunningham and dissed John Irving and Cormac McCarthy. She seems to have taken a vow to reduce the reputations of the best male American authors. Now, many reviewers have their tics, even the best. Clifton Fadiman, who was top dog in his time, had nothing good to say, nonetheless, for William Faulkner. Every time a Faulkner came out, he would trash it. But at least Fadiman waited until the book was in the stores. He didn't review two weeks ahead of time. That's my quarrel with Michiko. If a bad review is the first you read, it takes three good ones to overcome it. She knows exactly what she's doing.

JBM: Maybe it's because you once made a joke that "all women should be kept in cages."

NM: Thanks for bringing that one up. I believe I said it thirty-five years ago.

JBM: It's so absurd, it's funny. It's like saying, "The way to stop war is to castrate all men." No rational person would say that seriously. When you're talking to someone face-to-face and you make a joke like that, one sees the twinkle, one hears the inner laugh and knows you're kidding. But today we live in a world of sound bites. No humor allowed. I'm scared that good minds will be written off as insane or misogynists or racist—it's too easy to discredit anyone who may potentially be a threat.

NM: All right. My fear—not my attitude, but my fear—is that there's such a foul atmosphere now in America, such power-lessness for most of us—it's almost like the more power we have with the Internet, the less power we really have—you can feel this in the emptiness of so many blogs. There's a kind of dissipated fury in people today. They're frustrated, they're angry, and they are full of bad conscience, bad conscience among other things, that we're in Iraq, bad conscience that we're so passive about the fact that the top half of one percent of the country are pulling in—whatever they're getting—25 percent of the wealth of the country each year and not even being taxed for it properly. So of course, yes, public figures can be seriously reduced by making rash statements.

When that remark was made about women and cages, I was

talking to Orson Welles on television. The year, as I recall, was 1970, and Welles was most aware of women's lib. (It had not quite come into the public consciousness yet.) But he was ahead of me on that, and he kept going on and on as we spoke about how wonderful women are. I thought, "Here's Orson and myself, both been married and divorced a number of times. We know a lot about women, their positive sides and their negative corners, our lives have been altered profoundly by women, yet Orson is carrying on shamelessly about how sweet and lovely and good they are—as if nothing bad could ever come from a woman?" And I said, "Come on, Orson, they should be kept in cages." I didn't mean it any more than I would have if I said men should be kept in cages. I couldn't resist. Man, have I paid for that remark.

JBM: Anyone who knows you also knows it's absurd to think you're a racist or a misogynist. Any of that.

NM: No, I love women. Dare I say it? Maybe I love women more than I should. Who knows?

JBM: What concerns me is that even now you are scared to talk about this on tape.

NM: I'm not scared. I'm just tired of paying dues for it. For example, as a word, "Asiatics" is now a no-no. Totally politically incorrect. What a ridiculous fucking thing that is. Tell me, what do you call someone who is Asian or Asiatic?

JBM: Well, if you want to be truly politically correct, you need to get specific on where they are descended from: Chinese-American, Japanese-American, etc. If you are talking about everyone from Asian decent who was born in America, I suppose it would be Asian-American.

NM: Absurd. I would never make a remark even remotely racist about any group that's having trouble. I certainly wouldn't want to make an anti-black remark. Or an anti-Hispanic remark. But concerning the Japanese, it wasn't ugly. The Japanese are in no trouble now in America. They're the smartest kids we have in the schools. They may be a minority but they are a powerful one, and the nation of Japan is doing very well indeed. By the time the twenty-first century is over, if we get through it, Japan may be running the world. I don't know what they need their little antiracist organization to protect them for.

JBM: There's racism throughout this country. Putting a lid on which words are appropriate to use and which aren't is not going to solve the problem. It's like sitting on a blanket when the coals are still burning underneath.

NM: Some people are racist. Some are power-mad. People who are politically correct are not racist, but they sure are power-mad. When you get down to it, it's just as ugly as being racist.

JBM: Is there nothing to be done about it?

NM: It might take care of itself. Political correctness is not a satisfying activity when you get down to it. People may just get tired of mouthing it all the time. It's a boring way to live and a shaky method for shoring up one's psyche.

Marijuana

JBM: Why is the Bush administration fixated on a drug like marijuana, going so far as to overturn eleven states' rights in regard to even medicinal use of the plant, when the real drug problem in America is methamphetamines? Overturning states' rights? That's not conservative and it's certainly not my understanding of what the Republican Party is supposed to represent.

NM: To begin with, there's a great argument in America among conservatives themselves as to whether the Bushes are conservative. There is a relatively new magazine called *The American Conservative,* which to my mind is one of the more interesting periodicals in America. That is because they print so many different right-wing points of view—everything from strict and standard old-line conservatives to searching critiques of the war in Iraq. Most of the writers for *The American Conservative* are clearly opposed to Bush. They consider him a distortion of their values.

So one can't use Republicans and conservatives, as if they are one word, any more than you can speak of Democrats as a general species when the left wing and the corporate wing of the Democratic Party detest each other.

But you ask: why is it that the government itself has always been opposed to marijuana? Not just the Republicans—the Democrats as well. Over the last forty years, I can't think of a single administration, Republican or Democrat, that's come close to being promarijuana. I think it's for a simple reason: marijuana strikes high officials as intrinsically dangerous precisely because it's not physically disruptive enough. Rather, it's a little spooky. You can probably toke more marijuana in your life than drink alcohol. Alcohol destroys people much faster.

Now, I smoked marijuana for about five years. Loved it, smoked it intensely. I finally gave it up. Like any vice, there's a price you pay for what you get. In my case, I felt if I wanted to be a serious writer, I couldn't continue because—how to put it?—marijuana was foreclosing the future, anticipating the future, using up my future before it happened. I'd tear through the equivalent of two days' worth of my best perceptions in a pot high that lasted two hours. For the next couple of days I was blank. So I realized that if I wanted to be a writer, I couldn't keep on with it. I was eating up my novels before I could write them. For the sheer mind-joy of experiencing them all at once.

But I did get extraordinary insights while taking it, wonderful times. It's a rite of passage, if you will. I would never say to a young man or woman, "Don't take marijuana under any circumstances." One interesting thing is if you're not ready for it and don't want it, pot won't have much effect on you. I smoked it for a year, off and on, maybe three, four, five times in that first year, and nothing happened. I didn't have any reactions at all. Just felt a pall. A flatness. Everything in my psychic system was rejecting it (because I knew it would change my life). Then, on a given night, when a great deal was going on around me, there was a breakthrough. I suddenly had a much larger sense of what—of the universe, call it that. It's a spiritual drug. It changes the way you perceive existence. And that is why the political body, as such, is afraid of it. The country could tilt. It brings out suppressed contents in people, violence in some, and peace and love in others. A ruling society cannot enjoy allowing such metamorphoses to take place at random and at large. They don't even want people getting too loving. They aim to keep us on the straight and narrow.

JBM: I've never seen anyone's violence brought out by marijuana. Or heard of a guy getting stoned and beating his wife.

NM: You've never heard of it, but I have.

JBM: I spent a year in the trenches of the marijuana community when I worked at *High Times*. A wild, wacky year, let me tell you. But I did get to know that culture inside and out, good and bad, and I wouldn't say violence is the problem with the drug.

NM: Yes, but I don't believe it should be supported on that basis, that it brings out the love in people. Look at the crap that went on with LSD.

JBM: LSD and marijuana are completely different.

NM: Of course they are. But there was that whole thing with Timothy Leary? Turn on . . .

JBM: . . . tune in, drop out.

NM: Yes, full of the most self-indulgent crapola.

JBM: But that's not marijuana. LSD is a chemical that burns a hole in your brain. Marijuana grows from the earth.

NM: I couldn't agree more. But let's not pretend marijuana is just simple pleasure. It can bring out love in people. It can also bring out hate. You discover yourself. I discovered myself. I encountered angers and furies in me that I never would have known. One of the reasons I've never been psychoanalyzed is that I had those years on marijuana.

JBM: I'm not trying to say it's all-good. There's nothing that's all-good.

NM: Hell, no, there's nothing that's all-good or the world would tip. And then we'd all run to the same pharmacy.

JBM: While it may have brought out the rage in you, I think for most people it brings out their laziness. Their lackadaisical feelings. But it's not a drug to induce rage and riots on a massive scale.

NM: It . . . it brings to the surface what's in you. And if disorientation is under the lid, you'll be disoriented. If profound laziness is in you, if you really don't want to work or strive, it'll bring that out. If passivity is in you, it'll bring it to the fore. And, I'm telling you, from my own experience and the experience of many I know, if violence is in you, that'll come out too. Let's not pretend it's a one-way drug. It's as various as booze, for God's sake.

JBM: Booze can bring out violence in a nonviolent person. Or stir up violence that has been repressed—and intensify it.

NM: Exactly. The point is that booze is manageable as far as the powers that be see it. They have rules for it—driving while intoxicated—they feel they can control booze—and, of course, corporations that oversee the making of it can profit, which is a very big part of it. Mind you, I'm not gung-ho for the legalization of marijuana. I feel the moment it's made legal, the corporations will take it over and we'll never see simple marijuana again. We'll be offered all sorts of souped-up varieties—big ads for throat-easy menthol pot . . . vitamins in the grass, Viagratized High-Toke. . . .

(Laughter)

JBM: We would. There's no getting around that. At the same time, it's not hard to grow. You can plant seeds in most places and it'll spring up. I think that's one of the factors that keeps it off the corporate market. You'd have too many bootleggers.

NM: I'll bet you anything if they ever do legalize it, they'll make it much harder to grow. They'll start sending out stories about how the ground around your home could infest your home-grown with deleterious side effects—you watch.

JBM: The other tie-in with marijuana is hemp, which for me is the main reason it's illegal. Hemp is an alternative source of fuel and clothing. You can run a diesel car on hemp. It's a threat to the oil industry, the cotton industry, and to the alcohol and tobacco industries as well.

NM: That's yours. If you want to make a speech, I'll sit back.

JBM: I wouldn't dream of trying to make a speech to you. Thoughts in full pages are your end of this book. I'm content to question, listen, and on occasion, interject a thought or two.

NM: Ah, go fuck yourself.

(Laughter)

PART THREE

Mailer vs. Mailer:
A Talk About the Sport of Boxing*

By the time I was born, boxing had become the family sport. My father and his friends, my brothers and their friends, and my cousin and his friends went to the Gramercy Gym every Saturday morning, back in the early eighties, to spar. There existed an understanding that usually worked: they were not there to beat the piss out of each other, but to learn a little about themselves. Some may disagree, but in my father's world, boxing is truly one of the arts. This belief was fortified by the presence on most Saturdays of Jose Torres, who had been the light-heavyweight champion in the sixties.

* Originally appeared *in Stop Smiling,*Issue 20, April 15, 2005.

I was four years old at the time, but my dad let me come along on Saturdays and once even put me in the ring. Although I was considerably outsized by the forty-year-old man in the opposite corner, I had already come to the understanding that, when your time came, you just had to fight.

Of course, I was in no danger. However, someone happened to take a picture over the shoulder of the man in the opposite corner, capturing the look of terror in my four-year-old eyes. The expression on my face— I thought I was really going to have to fight this man—makes me smile even to this day, and I imagine, gave the guys at the club no end of amusement. It was not unlike the time my dad got down on his knees to box with me in our living room. I had just turned three at the time. He let me catch him one on the corner of his chin and immediately dropped to the floor, pretending I had knocked him out. I had, for a few hours, the gift of believing I possessed the best right hook in the world.

JBM: Which is your favorite weight class to watch and why?

NM: You know, generally speaking, you find greater skills in the lower weights. Sometimes you'll see flyweights who are extraordinary, or bantamweights. Lightweights and welterweights can be marvelous. Middleweights are a most exciting level to watch because, at their best, they approach the power of heavyweights but they still have top speed and skill. Heavyweights are usually the clumsiest of the fighters. Nonetheless, that's the division I find the most exciting. There is always interest in watching the big guys. Why? Because we always have this feeling: "What if I get into a fight with a man that big? How would I try to handle him?" I used to feel that way when I was younger. Now I just watch.

But all right, that's not the main reason. It's because heavy-weight champions live in a peculiar psychic state. A good heavy-weight can always beat a great middleweight. Why? It just seems to be true that a heavyweight who weighs, let's say, 200 pounds as opposed to the 160-plus of a middleweight—that's a five-to-four ratio in weight—has, nonetheless, a superior punching power of three-to-two. It's as if something happens in the chemistry of the body. The good middleweight usually has no chance against a heavyweight. The greatest welterweight in the world probably couldn't beat a mediocre heavyweight. Roy Jones, who was perhaps as classy a fighter, until his recent downfall, as anyone I've seen—the most inventive of all fighters—was, nonetheless, leery about entering the heavyweight class. All right, what makes it so fascinating? It's this. The heavyweight champion may be entitled to think of himself as the toughest guy in the world, but there could be some madman in Outer Mongolia who could kill him with his bare hands. You just don't know. So you live in this peculiar suspended psychic state: "Am I or am I not the toughest man in existence right now?" Add karate and other various martial arts. That increases the confusion. So, heavyweights are always on the edge of being a little crazy. Therefore, I love watching them fight. Serious boxing is always a study in character and discipline of a very rare sort and this demand is most dramatized at the heavyweight level.

JBM: I hate to tell you this, especially having grown up with boxing as the family sport, but I believe the Ultimate Fighting Championship proves that the toughest boxer in the world is far from the toughest man.

NM: Well, who are these ultimate fighters?

JBM: They come from all different disciplines, and can be paired with any weight class or other discipline of fighting. I've seen a sumo wrestler paired against a jujitsu master. The sumo didn't last two minutes. Likewise, I've seen a boxer, a heavyweight, fight the same jujitsu master, and he was done within one minute.

NM: But who was the boxer?

JBM: No one I'd heard of.

NM: It's different when you're up against a great champion.

JBM: How so?

NM: Hell, when you get a martial arts artist of the highest level fighting a great champion, you can't anticipate the amount of anxiety the martial arts guy is gonna feel. That's because the best professional heavyweights have gone through hell, literally, fights where it would have been easier to die than to continue. The exhaustion, the pain, may be heavier than any martial arts man ever had. My opinion is that if you've got a true boxing champion fighting a true martial arts champion, nothing would happen. The one time I saw something like that, Muhammad Ali was fighting some Japanese who was marvelous at, I don't know whether it was aikido, karate, tae kuan do, but it was dumb, it became the dumbest fight I've ever seen. The stupidest. It took place in Japan and I saw it on TV. The Japanese guy just got down on his back. Any time Muhammad Ali approached, he'd get kicked. The Japanese artist kicked him in the shinbone from his prone position, or on the thigh. There was no way for Ali to reach him. Fifteen rounds of that. Dullest damn thing I ever saw. The guy didn't dare get up once to try any vertical stuff on Ali. It was in no way a contest.

People who are not professional boxers but martial artists love the idea that they could take a fine boxer. But such boxers are fast—even the slower professionals are pretty damn speedy when you get down to it. The martial artist is not used to being punched repeatedly, let alone taking one good shot to the chin. John, I'd say let's leave this argument open. Let history decide.

JBM: Fair enough. Cus D'Amato, one of the greatest fight managers to have ever lived, talked about how a boxer must acknowledge their fear, not deny it. What are your thoughts on that?

NM: Well I knew Cus pretty well, particularly in the years when he was training Jose Torres and Jose was moving toward the light-heavyweight championship and then won it. I wouldn't say that Cus and I were close enough to be friends, but we liked each other and enjoyed each other's company. And Cus was a philosopher, the only boxing philosopher I ever encountered. But a true philosopher. And was always able to talk to his fighters at their level. He'd say to a beginner: "Look, my gym, Gramercy Gym, is two long flights up. By the time a kid like you, who wants to take up boxing but never boxed before, has climbed those two long flights of stairs"—and Cus would really emphasize with his voice how long those flights of stairs were, and I can tell you they were very long indeed—"by the time he's got to the top, he's overcome his first fear." Then he said, "When I get them ready for their first fight, I'd say, 'You're going to look across the ring and you're gonna be a little embarrassed because you're half-naked and it may be in your family that people don't walk around that way. But there you are; half-naked. Strangers are looking at you. Strangers who may not even like you. And you're looking at the guy you have to face. He looks so strong, so powerful. You're scared stiff when you eye him. Well, I'll tell you something. He's looking at you in the same way. He's just as scared of you. And that's something you gotta remember.' " That was the ABCs of it. But Cus could certainly get more advanced when it came to building a fighter's ego. I think there's almost a physiological necessity for a professional fighter to have a prodigiously powerful ego. Muhammad Ali is, of course, the example for all times. It's as if powerful egos can take more physical punishment. I really believe there is a physiological connection. Because why do we build an ego, any of us, for our own purposes, if it is not to be able to take daily blows, the disappointments, the cutting remarks, the way in which we may be ignored in certain places when we feel, "Hey, how can they do that? I'm important." And yet we're ignored. So the ego is there to drive us through to our objective. When it comes to boxing, that takes on prodigious dimensions. I remember when Jose was training for the light-heavyweight championship against Willy Pastranno, we sat there one night, Jose, Cus D'Amato and myself watching a fight on TV that Pastranno had had in London against a contender whose name I don't even remember now. He wasn't a very good fighter and Pastranno won the fight but didn't look all that good either. And Cus, afterward, made a small speech to Jose. He said, "Joe, I knew when we took on this fight that you would have no trouble with Pastranno. And, having watched you train very seriously for this one has reinforced my opinion, but I can tell you, having watched Pastranno in this fight, I know now as I look you in the face, I am also looking at the next light-heavyweight champion of the world." He said it in a big voice and Torres entered that fight with such confidence, that after the first round he came back to his corner and said to Johnny Manzanet, his trainer, who was a good, tough Puerto Rican, Torres said, "I am the next champion of the world." And Manzanet shouted at him, "Shut up, you got the whole fight to get through." *(Laughter)* At my end, I played a very small part for that one, maybe one part in five hundred. Which is I went out to watch Pastranno train, and came back to tell Jose, "He's only got one weapon. A wonderful jab. He's got a fabulous jab." I saw a very hard look come into Jose's eyes. So, I said, "If you can take that jab away from him, I don't know what he can do." The look got even harder. He was proud of his own jab. And in the first round, Jose came out and took the jab away from Pastranno, and dominated the fight all the way. They stopped it in the ninth.

JBM: Is a large ego necessary to overcome your fears?

NM: Not a large ego, a strong, focused ego. The ego has to be ready to match the intensity of a particular fear. A large ego might be the worst kind of ego to have as a fighter. The first time you get hit hard enough to feel real fear of your opponent, all the outlying regions of your ego are no good anymore. What's the use of saying to yourself, "I'm the best ballroom dancer in town. Or the greatest stud." That does you no good when you get hit in the kisser. That's when you need a rallying ground that only a particular ego can provide.

There's a famous story about Carmen Basilio, who was a very tough welterweight. One time, in a close fight, he got hit hard, and almost went down. I've never seen the position he got in before or since. His body sank to a horizontal but remained eighteen inches above the ground, because he was able to support himself on one bent leg, and held up by that beleaguered knee, he managed never to hit the canvas. Instead, he straightened up. It was an extraordinary effort. Later, one of the reporters asked, "Carmen, why didn't you go to the canvas for a count of eight and take a rest. You could have won the fight anyway." He said: "I didn't want to start no bad habits."

His ego said to him, "You don't hit the canvas. Nobody knocks you down." (He had, incidentally, never been knocked down in his career.) That's one of the differences between street fighters and professionals. One of the enormous differences. But then very few street fights are equal. One guy is usually bigger than the other, or one gang is stronger, so you can't often talk about equality in a street fight.

JBM: Mike Tyson started as a street fighter. Where does he fit into all this?

NM: I'd say he is the showcase for its difficulty. The balance, the transition from instinct to ego. He had in Cus D'Amato a better teacher than anyone around, but he also came out of an intolerably formless amoral scene—crazy background. He had prodigious talents and fine intelligence, but his ego, given the disproportions and imbalance of his spirit, lost the power to keep him in control of himself after Cus died. Many argue that it would have been the same if Cus had lived, that even he would not have been able to control Mike, but I'll bow out on that point. I don't know enough of what really went on before and after Cus's death.

JBM: What's your take on women boxing?

NM: Oh, as Richard Nixon used to say, I'm glad you asked that. (*Laughter*) You know, years ago when they started, women boxers were dreadful. They were as bad as the clumsiest oaf in a gym who throws roundhouse rights and roundhouse lefts until he's winded. The easiest punch to guard against is a roundhouse punch, right or left—you just put your gloves up around your ears and take note of them as they arrive. It's like stepping out of the way of a freight train when you have plenty of time. Your opponent gets winded very quickly throwing roundhouse punches. Anyway, the early women were so dreadful that I made the remark (and you know, nothing in those days was more valuable to me, you might say, than my private parts), but I said, "I'm half-tempted to have a sex-change operation. Because then I could be champion of the world." Just joking, but the point is that even though I was at best a mediocre amateur as a boxer, I knew enough to have been able to beat any one of those women at that time. Now it's no longer true. They've gotten much better. Much stronger, much faster, much tougher. Now, if I were still at my best I couldn't get in the ring with them. They've gotten very good. However, they're still a million miles away from top male fighters.

JBM: How is boxing different from other big sports—baseball, football, etc.?

NM: It's one against one. Boxing bears as much relation, therefore, to chess as to football. Because, in a chess game between two very good players, there is humiliation in losing. That humiliation is even greater in boxing. Of course, it's also true of all one-on-one sports. Tennis, for example. But boxing demands one thing more. Which is hard to name. It's almost like a certain courage of the blood that goes very deep. It's what attracts us to boxing. It's the side of boxing that's not too well understood by people who say, "I hate boxing. It's so brutal." It's the amount

of discipline and intelligence and restraint that goes into it.
Which is why I consider boxing a social good, not a social ill.
What would a lot of these kids do if there weren't professional
boxing and they couldn't make a living out of it? The answer is
that a lot of them would be likely to lead violent lives. You know,
when people have a little more violence in them than the
average, their lives take on all sorts of very difficult turns that
can't necessarily be solved by anger management courses. When
there's a lot of violence in a man, society can be grateful that
there are social ways that violence can be turned into an art
form. A kid who starts out as a very rough piece of work comes
to learn that there's something classy about getting good at
this boxing. It's a way for a violent man to begin to comprehend that living in a classic situation—in other words, living
within certain limitations rather than expressing oneself
uncontrollably—is a way to live that he didn't have before.
Because don't forget, that when you're violent and undisci-
plined, life is a nightmare. Any morning when you wake up
could be the morning where you go too far and hurt somebody
so badly that you're in the can, or you've killed them. Or you're
humiliated. Being macho is no fun. Because macho men have
to live for their triumphs and in terror of their humiliations,
and there's always another guy who's as macho as you are or

more. So boxing enables such kids to find a social form for themselves, where not only their strengths but their weaknesses can be appreciated. Where in effect they can be taught how to get rid of their weaknesses. They begin to learn that they have to show up on time, that they have to drill, that they can drink but they can't drink too much, they can take pot but they can't take too much because the head is too vulnerable after taking pot to get hit steadily through a sparring session. Some even begin to lead lives which enable them to have a little social standing outside of the gang. And that's a huge step. Because for every ten thousand who train every year, maybe a thousand ever make it to a reasonably high amateur level and five hundred to the professional level—I don't know what the numbers are. They're probably larger than that. But the point is, in the course of it, even if they don't succeed, they get a structure to their ego, and some measure of how tough they really are. One of the worst things about being tough is if you don't know how tough you really are, all you know is that you're kind of tough, that's scary. Your ego can be shattered by one episode. But if you go to the gym every day and are subtly humiliated every day by boxers who are better than you, you begin, in the course of it, to get better. You can make some kind of peace with much that's unsettled in yourself. Boxing gives proportion to the psyche. Now, there are penalties to it. You can end up less intelligent than when you started. That's obvious. On the other hand, I remember we had this boxing club we'd go to on Saturday mornings, and then after we'd go out to eat. We'd have hamburgers and beer, and I remember saying once, "Hey fellas, what would Saturday afternoon be like without a headache?" We all laughed, because it was true. On the other hand, it also occurred to me that this headache I had from boxing was not quite as bad as the headaches I used to have on mornings when I was hungover with a splitting headache. Which also gave me the next perception, which was that those of my friends who were drinkers were punch-drunk. Not from boxing. From booze. So you do pay a price for boxing, but you also pay a price for living. We all punish our bodies.

JBM: Is machismo a choice?

NM: Wait a minute. You started with the question, "How is boxing different from all other sports?" I think there's one way in which it is profoundly different. I, of course, never did enough boxing ever to be able to answer that question with authority, but I once heard Muhammad Ali speak of fighting Joe Frazier and saying, "Fighting him was like Death." And I knew what he meant. It was right after "The Thriller in Manila," which Ali won, but it was an unbelievably arduous, grueling, brutal fight. Several times within the course of that fight I think Ali felt that he was going to die if he didn't quit. So there is one element in boxing which is not unlike Evel Knievel's stunts–which is you can die doing it. Now, very few boxers die, but there can be a feeling in the middle of a fight when you're bad used up that to go on is very dangerous. Of course, there are other activities which are, as well. You see these kids who are on roller skates and do flip-flops high in the air. They could break their neck if they don't do it properly—or rock climbing. That can be exceptionally dangerous. The thing about boxing is that the danger is always there in the middle of prodigious punishment. And so it has its own éclat, it's own honor, its own dignity. Which is that in the middle of pain and grueling dull punishment, there is also honor. Which is very, very important to certain kinds of men, violent men. Because a violent man without honor is a dreadful piece of work. So, to summarize, let me say that one of the social values of boxing is that it enables men who have difficult and unbalanced psyches to be able to strive legitimately toward their own personal honor.

JBM: Is there a correlation between boxing and writing?

NM: A very small one, but it drew me to my interest in boxing. Which is: writers do suffer. But it's at long range. You print a sentence or write a paragraph that is going to offend certain people in certain places, and you know it. Of course, it's a tricky business. The people who it's going to enrage usually don't read books, they just hear about what you've done—which is usually worse. In any event, you may pay for it but you don't know how, when, or where; it's down the road. On the other hand, there does remain one huge similarity—just one; there are many, many differences, obviously—but the one huge similarity is that you've got to pull it out of yourself. Particularly when writing fiction. There comes a point where you really have to dig down into your own vitals in order to get something out there. And in that sense it can be killing. You can really feel that you are using yourself up as you write. And boxers have that same feeling. Sometimes they have to call up something deep down in themselves in order to continue. And also, if you are a serious writer, there is the added desire to be *more* than just a serious writer—to be a writer who makes a change in the history of one's time. That's a powerful motive. And when one feels that one is not successful at that, it is depressing, just as it is depressing for a prize fighter who comes to realize that his talent is not what he had hoped for. Big, but not big enough.

JBM: You once made a deal with Jose Torres where he would give you boxing lessons in exchange for writing lessons. How did that come about?

NM: Well, we did it the summer of 1973. It was after he'd retired from boxing. He'd been the light-heavyweight champion for a couple of years and then retired after losing a fifteen-round decision to Dick Tiger. He came up one summer to South Londonderry, Vermont, where I was staying. He was going to write a book. He wanted to become a writer. And I wanted to become much more of a boxer. I'd done a little, but I wanted to do more. So we'd box every day. Three two-minute rounds a day, every day. I once offended him greatly because he was trying to talk up my talents to some strangers and I said, "Oh, come on, Jose, I'm safer with you than I am with my sister." That got him so mad, he walked out of the room. Don't attack the credibility of a champion.

JBM: But you meant that he was good to the point you knew he wouldn't slip up and hurt you, right?

NM: Well, he was so good, so good. Still, we'd box. And very early on, he said, "Look, Norman, I was going to give you open targets to hit, but I can't do it. I spent my life being a defensive fighter."

He was one of the great defensive fighters of all time. Very hard to hit. In fact, he makes the remark, and I believe it, that he was only hit *hard* five times in his career. What he meant by hard, of course, is not what we mean. His measure was that he felt deranged by the punch, lost the high focus of his consciousness for a few seconds. That only happened to him five times in his entire career. So he wasn't going to give me openings to see if I could pop him. But what he did do is teach me a great deal about defense. Reflexively. He never gave instructions verbally. We'd spar and he'd see an opening—they were all over the place in the beginning—and he'd tap me. And then if I didn't protect myself better, the next time, he'd tap me a little harder. Very quickly, reflexes were built in. In time, I became a fairly good— at my level—a reasonably good defensive boxer. But teaching him to write . . . When it was all over, he obviously got the better of the deal. I went from being an absolute amateur boxer to somebody who had a few skills, modest skills. Whereas he became a much-published writer, and a pretty good one. Not a great one, but a good one. The thing is, it was a pleasure to teach him. The disagreeable aspect in teaching writing to most people is that most young writers are so sensitive that you don't want to ruin them with one harsh remark. So you baby them and then they are offended if you are tough on any one of their faults.

Whereas fighters—because they get hurt in the ring—have instructors who are brutal. They'll say, "You dumb fuckin' idiot! How many times I have to tell ya? Keep your left up! What do ya need? A string attached to your ear?" Stuff like that. And so they learn quickly. And they're meek while learning. Until they get to be very good. So I found that I could say what I wanted to Jose. And I enjoyed that. Teaching writing can be irritating. You're dealing with mistakes that are below your own level. And I wasn't a born teacher. That wasn't my enthusiasm, it was just part of the deal. So after a while I'd start yelling at him: "How many times I have to tell ya, that ya don't say the same thing twice in two sentences?" He'd say, "Yeah, okay, yeah right, Norman, yeah, I won't do it again." And he didn't. He learned. He was just damn good at it. Because Jose is also very bright, which was one of the reasons we were friends. It was a pleasure to discover someone with a totally different occupation that you could really talk to and he could talk to you.

JBM: Somehow I don't remember being coddled as a very young writer. Not by you.

NM: Well, I learned, this is the way to teach writing. Most talented young writers are babied and babied, and then they get their first reviews. They're aghast.

JBM: It can be crushing.

NM: They didn't know the world was that cruel.

Texas Hold 'Em

JBM: One of the many reasons I love no-limit Texas Hold 'Em is I find the balance between luck, skill, and bluffing a useful metaphor for life.

NM: Add guts to that. If you're playing at a level where you can't afford to lose the money and if someone's bluffing you out but you're not sure, it takes guts to stand up to them at that moment. So yes, it is a metaphor for certain kinds of life in America today. That may be why it's sweeping the country.

JBM: I'm hard-pressed to think of another game that has caught on as quickly as this.

NM: Can't think of one. By the time this book comes out, it may all have passed. I hope not—I love the game. In any event, right now it is immensely popular. You learn an awful lot about yourself as you play it. You even learn a good deal about your moods and how they shift. I've discovered that at my best, I'm quite a different player than at my worst. I'm able to take risks, I'm bold, I'm inventive, I see the possibilities and I'm willing to pursue them, I'm willing to lose, I'm willing to win, I gamble. I qualify this by saying I don't play for high stakes. If I were engaged at a level where I could lose my house on a given night, my guess is that I'd be a much smaller player, considerably more timid, and would lose anyway.

The thing I love about it at reasonable stakes is how you discover some of your strengths and weaknesses. There's a crux almost every night you play, some damnably dangerous moment. It's also a test of how you react to boredom. You can go through stretches of an hour or more when you don't get a decent hand. You can fall apart from the boredom of holding nothing but rags, and begin to do stupid things, take risks you shouldn't take, lose interest in the game. Or, you can have the fortitude to wait until you get a good hand. I think a lot of people in America are discovering themselves through this game. There's something wide open about it, which captures, I believe, a good deal of the old open optimism that this is a good country and can still rise above suburban pall and mall.

JBM: You're also tuning your instincts about how to read other people. There's real pleasure in guessing correctly how someone will react to a bet you've made. There's a touch of human understanding alive in it, and I feel that that is what we're all looking for, a sense of human connection, even as opponents. Perhaps poker has become so popular (in part) because it helps to counter the fear that the price we may be paying for our technology, is our humanity.

NM: Yes. And one of the entertainments of the game are those very rare moments when a legendary event does occur. We had an extraordinary hand in a recent game when three kings came up on the flop. The player who eventually won the game said, "You guys better watch out, I've got the fourth king in my hand." Well, there was no way of knowing if that was one of the two cards he held in secret. My hand combined with the five open cards gave me a full house. I was so sure I had the nuts, and he was on a bluff, and I was wrong. He did have the fourth king. So I lost half of what I was going to lose all night betting against him with the three kings I had on the board plus the two tens in my hand.

The point is, the three exposed cards of the flop can strengthen your two hole cards, or—and this is the heart of the game—you can pretend that it does by the size of your bet. Even if it doesn't. Neither you nor the other players you're dealing with can be certain whether you have the hand you pretend to have, or are merely representing that you do. Now, isn't that the way many a business lunch takes place in America? Over such a meeting, the two people involved are usually pretending to be stronger or weaker than they really are. For a variety of reasons. So, Hold 'Em brings us closer to the nitty-gritty of our daily trans-actions with others. So full we all are of a multitude of little lies and occasional big ones. That's one reason it has taken over. Such a quick panoply of intrigue and pretense.

Another reason that the game is so popular is that women are excellent at it. My wife is as good as I am. And she was never much of a card player before this. Every woman I've played with is good at it, and I think the reason is they are used to living at the edge of deception.

JBM: *(Laughter)*

NM: They are. In the past, they had to pretend so often to be something they were not, especially when with men, and so now they are able to see through men quickly, more quickly than we see through them.

JBM: To go back to the hand you were talking about, with the three kings on the flop, what was even crazier was that on the next hand, three aces came up on the flop!

NM: I certainly do remember.

JBM: We were all thinking, "My God, what are the chances of this? One in a million? One in two million?" And the guy who had won the previous hand says, "Fellas, I hate to tell you, but I've got the fourth ace." Well, I'm thinking, "There's no way in hell he can have the fourth ace." But I had a bad feeling in my stomach that made me superstitious enough not to bet. So I laid down a king and a jack, and everyone else folded, as well. The guy showed us his cards, and indeed, he had it, the fourth ace! The ace of spades, no less. I suggested he stop playing and go buy a lottery ticket.

NM: Even a legendary poker pro like Doyle Brunson says there's no such thing as luck, but you can look between the lines—he knows there's luck. And the mark of a great player is they'll play their luck—they know when it is with them and when she is not there. You have a sense of that.

JBM: Do you think it's possible to summon luck?

NM: No. Maybe some can—a few can. Maybe you can summon luck for a couple of days, which is usually what happens when you win a tournament. For skill alone is not enough in a very big tournament.

But I don't know that I want to stop here. Let me raise the blinds. I have spoken already of the relation of Texas Hold 'Em to a business lunch where the negotiators are often doing their best to represent themselves as weaker or stronger than they really are. Something of the same is true for athletes, except they offer the suggestion that they will run you down here even as they step there. The fact of the next move or its feint can always be seen on rerun in football, in baseball, basketball, hockey, boxing certainly, tennis, ping-pong, and any number of other sports. Athletes live in the back and forth of true and false representation.

Let me raise the blinds again. This condition is basic to half of all marriages in America. In no-limit Hold 'Em a bluff is not unlike cheating on your wife. It can be dangerous, expensive, awful in its inner feeling when you lose, and yet, how long could most marriages exist without the presence or the threat of infidelity? As Engels once wrote—I quote from memory—"When the Catholic Church discovered that infidelity was impossible to prevent, it made divorce impossible to obtain." But, then, Texas Hold 'Em without the bluff would be like a loveless marriage.

No, bless the boldness of the bluff. It even reconstitutes the dignity of the solid hands that you are ready to stay faithful to, as well as offering a return of the old American hope that a poor man can still become a millionaire and in his eyes the streets will be paved with gold if he stays away from the slots, roulette, twenty-one, and seeks instead to do the near-impossible—master the thrills of playing a strong game with a weak hand. What a joy to win with that and never bat an eye. So, you see, Hold 'Em is subversive.

JBM: Which institutions in American life are challenged by Texas Hold 'Em?

NM: The law: false representation is what, at worst, the law seeks to contain and, at best, looks to punish. Journalism: their honest hard-sought facts are often inaccurate, but to hand in a deliberate false representation is a copy-desk editor's nightmare. And, finally, the banks. The corporations. To them, false representation is much too close to embezzlement. It runs counter to the monolithic powers who still keep the American social machine more or less bolted down. America! Our spacious skies!

Existentialism—Does It Have a Future?[*]

I would say that Sartre, despite his incontestable strengths of mind, talent, and character, is still the man who derailed existentialism, sent it right off the track. In part, this may have been because he gave too wide a berth to Heidegger's thought. Heidegger spent his working life laboring mightily in the crack of philosophy's buttocks, right there in the cleft between Being and Becoming. I would go so far as to suggest Heidegger was searching for a viable connection between the human and the

* The following first appeared in *Libération*, June 2005.

divine that would not inflame too irreparably the reigning post-Hitler German mandarins who were in no rush to forgive his past and would hardly encourage his tropism toward the nonrational.

Sartre, however, was comfortable as an atheist even if he had no fundament on which to plant his philosophical feet. To hell with that, he didn't need it. He was ready to survive in midair. "We are French," he was ready to say. "We have minds, we can live with the absurd and ask for no reward. That is because we are noble enough to live with emptiness, and strong enough to choose a course which we are even ready to die for. And we will do this in whole defiance of the fact that, indeed, we have no footing. We do not look to a Hereafter."

It was an attitude; it was a proud stance; it was equal to living with one's mind in formless space, but it deprived existentialism of more interesting explorations. For atheism is a cropless undertaking when it comes to philosophy. (We need only think of Logical Positivism!) Atheism can contend with ethics (as Sartre did on occasion most brilliantly), but when it comes to metaphysics, atheism ends in a locked cell. It is, after all, near to impossible for a philosopher to explore into how we are here without entertaining some notion of what the prior force might have been. Cosmic speculation is asphyxiated if existence came into being *ex nihilo*. In Sartre's case—worse. Existence came into being without a clue to suggest whether we are here for good purpose, or there is no reason whatsoever for us.

All the same, Sartre's philosophical talents were damnably virtuoso. He was able to function with precision in the upper echelons of every logical structure he set up. If only he had not been an existentialist! For an existentialist who does not believe in some kind of Other is equal to an engineer who designs an automobile which requires no driver and accepts no passengers. If existentialism is to flourish (that is, develop through a series of new philosophers building on earlier premises), it needs a God who is no more confident of the end than we are; a God who is an artist, not a lawgiver; a God who suffers the uncertainties of existence; a God who lives without any of the prearranged guarantees that sit like an incubus upon formal theology with its flatulent, self-serving assumption of a Being who is All-Good and All-Powerful. What a gargantuan oxymoron— All-Good and All-Powerful. It is certain to maroon any and all formal theologians who would like to explain an earthquake. Before the wrath of a tsunami, they can only break wind. The notion of an existential God, a Creator who may have been doing His or Her artistic best, but could still have been remiss in designing the tectonic plates, is not within their scope.

Sartre was alien to the possibility that existentialism might thrive if it would just assume that indeed we do have a God who, no matter His or Her cosmic dimensions (whether larger or smaller than we assume), embodies nonetheless some of our faults, our ambitions, our talents, and our gloom. For the end is not written. If it is, there is no place for existentialism. Base our beliefs, however, on the fact of our existence, and it takes no great step for us to assume that we are not only individual, but may well be a vital part of a larger phenomenon which searches for some finer vision of life that could conceivably emerge from our present human condition. There is no reason, one can argue, why this assumption is not nearer to the real being of our lives than anything the oxymoronic theologians would offer us. It is certainly more reasonable than Sartre's ongoing assumption—despite his passionate desire for a better society—that we are here willy-nilly and must manage to do the best we can with endemic nothingness installed upon eternal floorlessness. Sartre was indeed a writer of major dimension, but he was also a philosophical executioner. He guillotined existentialism just when we needed most to hear its howl, its barbaric yawp that there is something in common between God and all of us. We, like God, are imperfect artists doing the best we can. We may succeed or fail—God as well as us. That is the implicit if undeveloped air of existentialism. We would do well to live again with the Greeks, live again with the expectation that the end remains open but human tragedy may well be our end. Great hope has no real footing unless one is willing to face into the doom that may also be on the way. Those are the poles of our existence—as they have been from the first instant of the Big Bang.

God, the Devil, and a Third Party

JBM: Why is it that, particularly in America, we feel the need to believe in a God that is all-good and all-powerful?

NM: One reason I would say is the very strong sense fundamentalists have that the devil is in them. This is what made them fundamentalists in the first place. Keep the lid on at all costs. A more formal theological approach to the devil is that God created him in order to give man free will to choose. Of course, that is exactly what fundamentalists don't want. Free will is a magnet that could put you into the devil's orbit if you don't watch out. So their prevailing idea is: "Give everything to Jesus; give up free will and respect all that is on high, follow the laws and, most crucial of all, don't have a mind of your own." They will be blessed if they are free of doubt, so free will is no problem—they have obviated it. They think those who reject Christ don't realize how bad hell is going to be. It's a wholly simplistic philosophy. But that's not your first question. You did ask why do Americans believe in God so much?

JBM: An all-powerful God. All-powerful and all-good.

NM: In previous ages, when civilization was younger, nature was always before us. It was difficult *not* to think of a God who was all-powerful. My God, if you had a bad storm outside, it could blow your hut away. Most organized religions, indeed, if not all, share their roots in that fear of God. At the same time, today, technology has not only reduced our fear of God but has thereby created a large migration away from those who believe that God is almighty. One of the ironies we've hardly touched on is that the corporation with its love of technology is now allied with fundamentalism and its essential distrust of technology. The two of them march down the road together, hand in hand, like a very badly married couple.

JBM: What do they have in common?

NM: Oh, the desire to sit in judgment, the wish to live on high—one looks to be economic top dog, the other to loll in eternal heaven looking down on us unregenerate sinners. But there's the implicit sense that the suits and the fundamentalists need each other to maintain power. So it is like a powerful marriage where neither can bear the mate. Yet, the mate is necessary to one's ambitions.

JBM: What's your personal take on God? It's hardly blind faith.

NM: I believe in a God who is not all-good and all-powerful, but doing the best He or She can do. I've said this over and over again for some years. Before, when we were talking, you asked where is the hope? I felt my answer was incomplete when I said, "You just do the best you can."

Of course, there is more to it than that. There is politics after all. For example, I think the Democratic Party needs to be renovated from top to bottom. And certainly not by me at the age of eighty-two. Here I am on the sidelines saying that the Democratic Party has to be renovated—yeah, three cheers. But I do think your generation can do a lot in that direction. The Democratic Party, however, may have to lose some twenty or thirty years rehabilitating itself. If it doesn't, it may always be the second party. Because they are linked with the corporation. Until they separate themselves, until they recognize there's two kinds of capitalism—each opposed to the other—the capitalism of the corporation and that of small business. The latter is creative and the first is a totalitarian leviathan. When it comes to such large government—whether private or public (for their similarities can prove closer than their differences)—I'll take socialism over corporatism. At least the first is not slavishly dependent on market hype. Of course, at this moment in our history, socialism is a no-no. One of the reasons socialism failed in many countries and endures in some as a set of institutions—neither exciting nor awful—is precisely because those governments offer no sense of an existential God. To those of us who look for a better world, the concept of an existential God could rejuvenate a number of important needs, including our desire for a vibrant inner life that is not locked in dogma. We might, thereby, be able to hope, even to believe that God also wants a better world. Once we relinquish the cosmic supercharger, the power-trip that God is almighty and all-good, but rather is looking to do the best He or She can do, we can take inner life from that. Why? Because then we are part of it, and so perhaps are doing more for God (and for ourselves) than singing His praises whenever we are full of hysteria. Instead, we can feel an active, even vital relationship. We look to help God and, on occasion, we will also betray God, even as God, like a tired general, doesn't always come to our aid when we are beleaguered. Nonetheless, a sense that there can be collaboration between God and ourselves does offer the potential to create in the future a religious party of the left that is able to contest the religious panjandrums of the right.

JBM: Why does it have to be the Democrats? Why can't we create a third party that is not tied into the corporation the way the Democrats are? I mean, there's so much money funneled into the Dems—as we saw in this last election. I don't understand what is keeping some of that money from starting a viable third party.

NM: If a viable third party started and it grew and it showed signs of growth, I'd be for it. The Democratic Party is, after all, Republican-Lite, and will, doubtless, remain half-inert, and we will continue to invest emotion in political figures who are attractive in the beginning and disappoint us in the end. I'm thinking specifically of Clinton and Kerry.

JBM: Do you think it's a possibility that God is not eternal, but has a lifespan as well, even needs to be replaced at certain times?

NM: Totally beyond my compass. I do think that God, at the very least, has been evolving—if there's any real evidence to take from the Old and New Testaments, Jehovah is certainly a good step back of Christ. The Jesus who showed himself then has never really appeared again. The various churches developed their different notions of the Son, and organized their tenets into schemes of domination. Whereas Christ, to me, was an existential God. That's why I wrote *The Gospel According to the Son*. Christ, for my modest version, was doing the best that he could do. He was not all-powerful. He was often bewildered. Christ saw himself as the Son of God, but he hardly knew why He had been chosen, and hardly knew when or why He was successful. To repeat, He was doing the best he could do under difficult circumstances. An existential God, if ever there was one.

So I start from that, which is, of course, a fiction, an assumption, taken directly from another fiction, the New Testament. Nonetheless, my intent in writing that novel was precisely to stay true to the New Testament as far as the facts were concerned, the so-called facts, that is, kept it with all the miracles, kept it void of sex with Mary Magdalene, kept it the way it was presented to us in the Synoptic Gospels of Mark, of Matthew, and Luke. The Gospel of John presents too many problems because he is usually at odds with the other three concerning the order of events, and I wanted to see what I could come up with in the way of a story that made sense. Mind you, I believed in an existential God before I ever started that book. If I have a faith it is that God is looking to make the best creation possible, against great odds. I believe there is a devil opposing Him. I believe that in the eye of the cosmos, God is not all-powerful, not at all. God is a god among the many gods out among the galaxies, and they are all vying to develop their vision of existence rather than accept visions from other gods opposed to them. The lineaments of this speculation are more beautiful and more exciting to me than the notion of a God who rules over everything and sends us to heaven or hell depending on whether we did or did not break one of his Almighty laws.

JBM: Since it takes a man and a woman to create a child, does it not make sense that it would take at least two opposite but equal forces to create our universe? Or perhaps the birth of existence came through a melting pot of forces. A galactic orgy, if you will. You once called me a pagan for my personal beliefs, which I find interesting because they seem in accord with what you're saying now.

NM: What are your personal beliefs? I ask this twenty-seven years after your birth.

JBM: There's a number of what I would call spirits that I pray to. Spirits I go to when someone I love is truly in need of help. These spirits are not all-powerful, but if they are so inclined, can offer a great deal of help. At times I have even believed their help was miraculous.

I see myself as fighting for their team. I live my life in accordance with what I believe is their code. And this code happens to be in accordance with the teachings of Jesus and the basic underlying philosophy found in most religions: be good to your neighbor, don't take more than you need, give as much as you can, and protect the ones you love. I would add: work hard, and have a kick-ass good time doing it. When I first told you I pray to these spirits, it seemed to bother you.

NM: I'm not a great believer in prayer. I've never understood it. Maybe that's a sizable lack in me. My feeling has always been that our God, whether large or small, has so much to contend with, is so busy, so overstressed, that the last thing the Lord wants to hear is a tearful plea or even a reasonable request from somebody who needs something. My presumption is that He knows it already, more or less.

So my feeling is whatever strength God has, whether immensely more powerful than I think, or not as powerful as I hope, nonetheless, under it all, God is aware of us, very aware of us.

JBM: Why? Why are you so sure?

NM: Because we are part of God. Just as God is part of us. You have any number of religions that share one belief anyway—which is that each of us contains within us a light, a spark, an illumination of God.

JBM: Are you aware of what's going on with your nine children if they never bring it to your attention?

NM: No. That's another element of it, I have to admit. If you bring it to my attention, then I'm more aware of it and I do react. Maybe in that sense I'm dead wrong on prayer.

JBM: Well, there are certain things you sense, or know. But overall you can't expect any creator to be completely aware of its creation's needs all of the time.

NM: Maybe it's just that I would like God to have a little more sense of the whole, and be a little more alert and aware of what's going on than I am in relation to my children. (*Laughter*)

JBM: But you keep saying God is just doing the best He or She or both can do.

NM: In that case, prayer may be necessary. I have to admit. You could argue it both ways.

JBM: I'll settle for that. What thought would you like to end this book on?

NM: My last remark is sufficient. Let us be ready to argue it both ways. No authorities exist who have certain knowledge. As Nietzsche once said, "All priests are liars." Yes, and so are all the rest of us. Often, I believe that we are here to leave the world with better questions than the ones with which we came in—dare I say it—maybe that is what God desires the most—that He or She can be stimulated by what can be learned from us.

Finis